Small Group Study

VOLUME 3

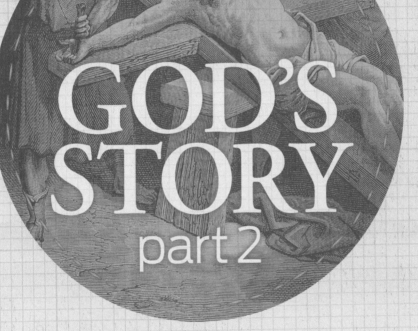

GOD'S STORY
part 2

The New Testament

THE
GOSPEL
PROJECT
FOR ADULTS

LifeWay | Adults

...tetzer General Editor Trevin Wax Managing Editor

© 2012 LifeWay Press®

No part of this work may be reproduced or transmitted in any form or by any means, electronic or mechanical, including photocopying and recording, or by any information storage or retrieval system, except as my be expressly permitted in writing by the publisher. Requests for permission should be addressed in writing to LifeWay Press®, One LifeWay Plaza, Nashville, TN 37234-0175.

ISBN: 978-1-4300-2536-8
Item: 005584681

Dewey Decimal Classification Number: 220.07
Subject Heading: BIBLE—STUDY \ THEOLOGY—STUDY \ GOSPEL—STUDY

We believe that the Bible has God for its author; salvation for its end; and truth, without any mixture of error, for its matter and that all Scripture is totally true and trustworthy. To review LifeWay's doctrinal guideline, please visit *www.lifeway.com/doctrinalguideline*.

Unless otherwise noted, all Scripture quotations are taken from the Holman Christian Standard Bible®, copyright 1999, 2000, 2002, 2003, 2009 by Holman Bible Publishers. Used by permission. • Scripture quotations marked (*The Message*) are from *The Message* by Eugene H. Peterson, copyright © 1993, 1994, 1995, 1996, 2000, 2001, 2002. Used by permission of NavPress Publishing Group. All rights reserved.

To order additional copies of this resource, write to LifeWay Church Resources; One LifeWay Plaza; Nashville, TN 37234-0113; phone toll free (800) 458-2772; fax (615) 251-5933; email *orderentry@lifeway.com*; order online at *www.lifeway.com*; or visit the LifeWay Christian Store serving you.

Printed in the United States of America.

Adult Ministry Publishing
LifeWay Church Resources
One LifeWay Plaza
Nashville, Tennessee 37234-0175

Table of Contents

Writers

Part 1: Jesus' Life and Ministry

Keith Whitfield lives in Wake Forest, North Carolina, with his wife and two children. He teaches Christian Theology at Southeastern Baptist Theological Seminary. Before joining the faculty at Southeastern, he spent two years teaching and training church planters in Nashville, Tennessee, and five years as a pastor in southeast Virginia.

Part 2: God's New Covenant People

Joey Jernigan serves as a lead pastor at Lanier Islands Community Church in Buford, Georgia. He also teaches as an assistant professor at Liberty University Online. He is married to Lindsay, and they have three daughters, Ella, Eden, and Emma.

Part 3: Living in Light of the Returning King

Afshin Ziafat resides with his wife, Meredith, in Frisco, Texas, where he is the lead pastor of Providence Church. He is also the founder of Afshin Ziafat Ministries and travels nationally and internationally proclaiming the gospel. Afshin speaks weekly at Vertical Bible Study at Baylor University in Waco, Texas. He also partners with Elam Ministries and travels into the Middle East regularly to train Iranian pastors.

The Gospel Project

Introduction

Some people see the Bible as a collection of stories with morals for life application. But it is so much more. Sure, the Bible has some stories in it, but it is also full of poetry, history, codes of law and civilization, songs, prophecy, letters—even a love letter. When you tie it all together, something remarkable happens. A story is revealed. One story. The story of redemption through Jesus. **This is** *The Gospel Project.*

When we begin to see the Bible as the story of redemption through Jesus Christ, God's plan to rescue the world from sin and death, our perspective changes. We no longer look primarily for what the Bible says about us but instead see what it tells us about God and what He has done. After all, it is the gospel that saves us, and when we encounter Jesus in the pages of Scripture, the gospel works on us, transforming us into His image. **We become God's gospel project.**

Core Values

Deep, but Not Dry

We believe it's best to expect a lot out of those who attend a small group. We don't need to go only as deep as the least knowledgeable person in the group. We may have to "cut up the meat" for new believers and make sure the truth is accessible, but the important thing is that everyone has been fed and is sufficiently nourished.

Christ-Centered

God is the primary Actor in the grand narrative of Scripture, and the gospel of Jesus Christ is the climax of this story. We approach the Old Testament as Jesus did: all the Scriptures testify to Him. We approach New Testament ethics and commands as implications that flow from the gospel—Christ crucified and raised.

Story-Focused

Being Christ-centered naturally brings our focus to the overarching story that the Bible tells in four parts: Creation / Fall / Redemption / Restoration. This helps us connect the dots in the great story that tells the truth about our world and provides a hope-filled outlook on our world because of the future God has promised.

Mission-Driven

Telling the story of the Bible is impossible without leading to mission, as the gospel reveals the heart of our missionary God and His desire to save people of every tribe, tongue, and nation. Keeping a focus on how the gospel leads us to mission is a crucial aspect of how we apply the Bible to our lives.

Joy to the World

Part 1

JESUS' LIFE AND MINISTRY

In the fullness of time, God Himself, in the person of His Son, came to earth and took on human nature. In His teaching, Jesus proclaimed the arrival of God's kingdom. In His miracles, Jesus displayed the compassion and power of the kingdom. In His death on the cross, Jesus took upon Himself the punishment that we deserve for our rebellion against God. In His resurrection, Jesus was victorious over sin and death. Now Jesus is at the right hand of God the Father, where He reigns as the saving ruler of God's kingdom.

Chapter 1

The Incarnation

The Coming of the Messiah-King

For more than a century now, the mysteries of Sherlock Holmes have captivated teenagers and adults alike. Even in our high-tech, quickly changing world, the Victorian-era detective's popularity remains high. Although Holmes was not the first, he has become the most famous of all fictional detectives. His quick wits, keen observations, and instinctive knowledge challenge the audience to try their own hand at beating Holmes in solving the mystery. The Holmes stories draw you in. The suspense grabs you. You become a part of the drama because you have been led to seek answers.

At the beginning of our study of the New Testament, we are greeted by the four Gospel writers—Matthew, Mark, Luke, and John. In their own particular ways, they want to draw us into a story as well. The question at the heart of the Gospels is the same question posed in the Christmas carol by William Chatterton Dix—"What Child Is This?"

The Gospels intend to tell us who Jesus is. In these stories, we see the religious leaders trying to figure Him out. A Jewish king was threatened by His birth, and a Roman centurion was amazed by His death. His disciples followed Him, encountered His power, and continued to have their expectations challenged.

In this chapter, we will look at the opening verses of John's Gospel and discover some of the most important words in Scripture on the identity of Jesus and the reason He came. As we explore the purpose and the way Christ came to earth, we will see what it means to be like John the Baptizer—a faithful witness to the grace of God shown to us in Jesus Christ.

The identity of the King who has come (John 1:1-5)

1 *In the beginning was the Word,*
and the Word was with God,
and the Word was God.
2 *He was with God in the beginning.*
3 *All things were created through Him,*
and apart from Him not one thing was created
that has been created.
4 *Life was in Him,*
and that life was the light of men.
5 *That light shines in the darkness,*
yet the darkness did not overcome it.

"In the beginning..." The Gospel of John opens with three words that immediately take us back to the first words of the Bible. Remember how the story began? God created the heavens and the earth, but the earth was formless, void, and covered with darkness (Gen. 1:1-2). The rest of Genesis 1 shows how God formed the earth, filled it with good things, and gave it light. Once finished, He judged His work to be "very good" (v. 31).

The world didn't remain that way, though. Humans rebelled (Gen. 3), and sin spread to everyone. God's assessment of creation changed. Creation was no longer as God intended it to be, and the judgment of death came upon the earth. But God's purposes for His creation were not finished. So He called Abraham and Moses and formed a people for Himself, a people through whom He would bring redemption from sin and death.

A primary theme of the Old Testament is that the people of God are stuck in disobedience. Another theme is that God promises to make things right for His people. At the close of the Old Testament, Israel has returned from exile, but things are not yet made right. Ezra painted a post-exile picture of hope and longing, joy and weeping (Ezra 3:10-13). The post-exile prophets (Haggai, Zechariah, and Malachi) condemned Israel for their disobedience and pointed to a time when things would be different. The end of the Old Testament looks forward to a day when freedom from sin and death will come to the people of God. That's the point in the story where the Gospel of John starts.

In the passage above, we see how John began by describing the divine nature of Jesus. His descriptions draw us into a web of abstract images and allusions. There is a mystery around Jesus and His coming, and John used the title "the Word" and the images of light and life to tell us about Him.

In the opening verses of John's Gospel, we see how the work of God in creation shapes the way John tells the story of the salvation that comes through Jesus. After the fall into sin, God's creation was invaded by darkness. But here we are introduced to the Word who took the formlessness of the first creation and made it "very good." He comes now to re-create. Jesus is going to remake His broken world.

While John does not explain the origin of "the Word" as a title, he does expound on the identity and nature of this Word. The Word shares in the divine nature. He is God (John 1:1). Yet He exists as a Person distinct from the Father—He is with God (v. 1). The Word created all things (v. 3). The Word is life (v. 4). The Word has sovereign power (v. 5).

John, under the guidance of the Holy Spirit, searched to find just the right title for Jesus. "The Word" captures the idea of God in action, revealing Himself in creation and in salvation. He speaks and things happen. As we uncover what John means in these verses, something interesting happens. Unlike a detective in a mystery novel, we don't discover the identity of this King through observation, deductive reasoning, and intuitive insights. The identity of God is *revealed* to us.

The witness to the King who has come (John 1:6-9)

6 *There was a man named John*
who was sent from God.
7 *He came as a witness*
to testify about the light,
so that all might believe through him.
8 *He was not the light,*
but he came to testify about the light.
9 *The true light, who gives light to everyone,*
was coming into the world.

The Word is the self-expression of God, and when He comes, He comes with power to overcome darkness. But we discover here that God sent a man to bear witness to this light. How curious! Notice how John invites us into this story. After telling us about the Word, he introduces us to a prophet.

John the Baptizer stood in a long line of witnesses. The Old Testament is full of voices that reminded Israel of God's covenant promises to send a King who would save His people. Isaiah told us He would save through suffering (Isa. 53). Ezekiel proclaimed that life would come to the dead (Ezek. 37). Jeremiah looked to the power of a new covenant that would reform the hearts of God's people (Jer. 31).

John the Baptizer joined these ancient voices. The Gospels describe John as a locust-eating prophet who spent years baptizing people in the wilderness. John was the one who baptized Jesus and declared Him to be the Lamb of God, who takes away the sin of the world (John 1:29).

Like a candlestick holds a candle, John held up the light as he called people to prepare for the coming of their salvation (Ps. 132:17). His ministry was to stir in the hearts of God's people a holy anxiousness to see the fulfillment of God's promises. People came out to the wilderness to meet him. They came to identify with the rebellious, exiled nation, and they were baptized as a sign of repentance and faith in the coming salvation.

This is an interesting place for John, the Gospel writer, to introduce the Baptizer. Verse 5 is about the true light, and verse 9 picks up that theme again. But sandwiched between these two sections on light, John shifts attention to John the Baptizer. Why? It's because John wants to introduce a major theme that will be developed throughout this Gospel. It's the theme of *witness*, and it culminates in John 20:21 when Jesus tells His disciples that He is sending them just as the Father sent Him.

John directs our attention to the value and significance of a witness. Witnesses bear testimony to something. It's important to remember the subject of our testimony. Sometimes it is tempting to think that our story is the subject of our witness. But John reminds us in verse 8 that the Baptizer was not the light, and if *he* wasn't the light, *we* certainly aren't the light either. This reminds us that our personal testimony (while a great demonstration of the power of the light) is not the point. Instead, we are to be a witness to the true light—Jesus. His story is more important than ours.

One of Jesus' disciples, Peter, refused to bear witness to Jesus on the night He was betrayed. But by the end of the Gospel of John, we find Peter accepting his calling to be a witness. Jesus described Peter's coming martyrdom. But before the dark day when Peter witnessed to the light by his death, he would stand on the Day of Pentecost and bear witness to 3,000 people, not by telling his personal story of failure and redemption but by telling the story of Jesus.

The purpose of the King who has come (John 1:10-13)

10 *He was in the world,*
and the world was created through Him,
yet the world did not recognize Him.
11 *He came to His own,*
and His own people did not receive Him.
12 *But to all who did receive Him,*
He gave them the right to be children of God,
to those who believe in His name,
13 *who were born,*
not of blood,
or of the will of the flesh,
or of the will of man,
but of God.

Do you notice something mysterious about the light John describes in this passage? The light overcomes the darkness, right? But when He comes into the world, He is not seen. How can this be? A light has come into darkness but cannot be seen. Impossible! John crafted his words purposefully for us to see how outrageous this is and then to provoke us to ask the question "How do we see the light?"

John made two points about human blindness to God's light. First, he said the world doesn't recognize its Creator. We owe our existence to Him, and we were made for Him, but we've failed to recognize Him (Rom. 1:18-23; Col. 1:16; Rev. 4:11).

Notice what comes next. Referring to the Jewish people, John said Jesus' own people did not know Him. Even though they had received the covenant promises, the law, the witness of the prophets, and the promise of the Messiah, they rejected Him when He came (John 5:39-40). Their eyes were blinded and their ears were deaf to the truth.

So Jew and Gentile alike, both created in God's image for His purposes, are separated from Him and blind to His light. A bleak picture.

Thankfully, John took a turn in verse 12 with the word "But." This little word is strategically located in a number of places in Scripture: "No one will be justified in His sight by the works of the law...*But* now, apart from the law, God's righteousness has been revealed" (Rom. 3:20-21); "And you were dead in your trespasses and sins...*But* God, who is rich in mercy...made us alive" (Eph. 2:1-5).

John drew a similar contrast. The Light came into the world, yet it did not recognize Him. Even His own people did not receive Him. *But* some did receive Him. The contrast John made draws our attention to the fact that relationship with God involves receiving Jesus, believing in His name. And yet salvation is God's work, to which we respond. John makes that point by telling us that these people are born not of blood, the will of the flesh, or the will of man; rather, they become children of God by being born of God (John 1:13). When we receive Jesus, God gives us a new identity. We are called children of God (v. 12).

So what is the point and purpose of Christ's coming? To bring salvation and form a new family. Christ came to open the eyes of the spiritually blind. Earlier, we saw that we are called to be witnesses to Jesus. Now, in these verses, we see why witnessing is possible. Jesus changes us. His coming to us frees us to go to others.

The way the King has come (John 1:14-18)

14 *The Word became flesh*
and took up residence among us.
We observed His glory,
the glory as the One and Only Son from the Father,
full of grace and truth.
15 *(John testified concerning Him and exclaimed,*
"This was the One of whom I said,
'The One coming after me has surpassed me,
because He existed before me.'")
16 *Indeed, we have all received grace after grace*
from His fullness,
17 *for the law was given through Moses,*
grace and truth came through Jesus Christ.
18 *No one has ever seen God.*
The One and Only Son—
the One who is at the Father's side—
He has revealed Him.

It's hard to keep kids away from wrapped presents under the Christmas tree. They battle the constant temptation to peek through a little rip in the paper here or there. They want to know what's inside, so they try to catch even a small glimpse of the box so they can figure out the clues as to the contents.

Like a detective novel that gradually shows you more and more, the prologue to John's Gospel now introduces us to Jesus Christ by name. We've already seen that the Word is divine and eternal and that He created all things. We've seen that He came to the world, but the world did not receive Him. We've seen that some receive Him—those who are born of God (or born again). But up until this point, John has not revealed to us the identity of the Word and how the Word comes to the world. In these last few verses, our questions are answered.

The most staggering Christian claim is that Jesus of Nazareth was God made man. When He came, He came to dwell with His people. Some translations render the key thought in verse 14 as "dwelt among us." A popular paraphrase renders it "moved into the neighborhood" (*The Message*). The HCSB translates it as "took up residence among us." This image recalls the Old Testament tabernacle, which God set up as a place where the priest would enter on behalf of the people once a year—a place where sinners met with God and a place that symbolized God's desire to dwell with His people.

Through the miracle of God becoming man, we see who God is and what He is like. The box under the Christmas tree is unwrapped, and we are amazed at the gift inside! John says we observed His glory as the One and Only Son from the Father, full of grace and truth (John 1:14).

God demonstrated grace in former times but superseded that grace and manifested the fullness of grace and truth in sending the Son (Heb. 1:1-3). The law given to God's people in the Old Testament was a gracious gift, but in Jesus Christ, God manifested greater grace. Moses was the servant through whom the grace of the law was given. Jesus Christ is the Person through whom grace upon grace is given (3:5-6).

Christ's glory was manifested in many ways. The transfiguration of Jesus is one of the more dramatic demonstrations of His glory (Matt. 17). Another instance would be the raising of Lazarus from the dead (John 11). But the greatest display of the glory of God in Christ would be His death, burial, and resurrection (John 12:27-28). He came to live. He came to die. He came to live again.

Conclusion

Will we see the glory of God in the face of Jesus (2 Cor. 4:6)? God designed the gospel and sent His Son so that we can see His glory. John wrote his Gospel to help us see how God, by sending His Son, makes Himself known to us. The goal of this Gospel is to demonstrate to us that Jesus is the Son of God and that He accomplished everything God sent Him to do. Life is found in Him (John 17:1-3).

John answered William Chatterton Dix's question—"What Child Is This?" The child is Jesus the Messiah, God in the flesh. Like a great storyteller leading us to the climax of the plot, John rooted his readers in the narrative of the Old Testament and then introduced the One who came to make God the Father known.

In the Person of our Lord Jesus Christ, God incarnate, the invisible God is now visible to us. Jesus came to explain to us—to teach us—about the goodness and glory of the Father. Moses longed to see God more fully and was granted a partial glimpse (Ex. 33:17–34:7). In Christ we see God dwelling among us in human flesh (Col. 1:15). It is more than we could ever have hoped for! It is more than we shall ever be able to grasp! It is a wonder that will inspire our worship throughout time and eternity.

Devotions

THE MISDIRECTION

It is hard to know what is wrong until we know what is right. We often think, in fact, that we are right when we are wrong. When we are really lost, there is no way for us to find our own way. We need directions to get back on the right path.

God has revealed His plan for everything. His plans orient us and help us see what is wrong in our lives. His path for all things is revealed in Colossians 1:16: "For everything was created by Him, in heaven and on earth, the visible and the invisible, whether thrones or dominions or rulers or authorities—all things have been created through Him and *for* Him." We were created by God to live a God-ward life. Yet God's plan for creation has been misdirected—not by God, but by us! We have taken a wrong turn.

The misdirected path started just after creation. Adam and Eve decided to rebel against God's good instructions. God, in mercy and judgment, sent them away from the place He had ordained to dwell with His people. Following the aftermath of this through Scripture, we see that humanity is unable to recover the God-ward life. We have rewritten Colossians 1:16. Our version goes something like this, "For everything was created by Him...through Him and for *us.*"

The greatest temptation we face is to live for ourselves. Even our religious devotion can be twisted by this lure. We use our service, our obedience, and our sacrifice to win favor, to ease our guilt, and to earn praise from others.

The good news is that God has done something to win our hearts back to living for Him. In Jesus' life and ministry, we discover that God is *for us*, and through the gospel we can be changed and live *for Him* (2 Cor. 5:14-15).

Pause and Reflect

1   Can you think of a time when your emotions and desires have made it difficult to consider God's design?

- -

2   How does the good news that God is for us in the Person of His Son make a difference?

A Redirecting Promise

God promises to redirect the course of His people: "This is the LORD's declaration...I will make a new covenant with the house of Israel" (Jer. 31:31).

After the fall into sin, God promised a solution. He promised Adam and Eve that One would come to conquer, crushing the head of the Deceiver (Gen. 3:15). The details of God's promise are filled out in the calling of Abraham and the promise that He will make Abraham into a great nation. After He rescued His people from slavery, God promised them, "Now if you will listen to Me and carefully keep My covenant, you will be My own possession" (Ex. 19:5).

But the story of Israel is not one of obedience but of disobedience. So God said He was going to do something that would make a difference. When the Lord spoke in Jeremiah 31, He put Himself on the line. He said, "I will do what needs to be done."

Do you believe this? In your desperate need to be redirected, where do you look for clarity? Do you look inside to see how you feel? Or to how much confidence you have in your ability? Or do you look outside toward a friend? A spouse? A parent?

God does not redirect us first in where we look. First, He redirects us in what we *hear*. God says, "Hear Me, I will do the work." Then He says to look. But He does not intend for us to look inward or outward to another person. He tells us to look at the works of His hands as evidence of the trustworthiness of His Word (see Jer. 31:35-36).

Pause and Reflect

1   Where do you look when you need clarity?

- -

2   What does it mean to hear the truth of the gospel first and then to look?

A New Direction

The Greek philosopher Heraclitus once said, "Everything flows, nothing stands still."

While this statement has to do with change being unavoidable, it also captures a spiritual truth. Spiritually, we are never standing still. We live for something. It's unavoidable.

God made us to live for Him, but we get misdirected and live for someone else. But as we discover in John 1, God does something to change our direction, and our transformation happens because of the Word.

God redirects us, and He gives us the right to be called "children of God" (John 1:12). And when God redirects us, He sends us in a new direction with a new purpose. John 20:21 says, "As the Father has sent Me, I also send you."

We are sent. We are called to join God in His mission. We learn in John 1 that God sent His only Son to make Himself known to the world. By following John the Baptizer's example, we can join in on His mission.

Remember John the Baptizer's words? He said: "I am not the Messiah" (1:20); "I am a voice of one crying out in the wilderness" (1:23); "Here is the Lamb of God, who takes away the sin of the world!" (1:29).

Like John the Baptizer, we are sent to be witnesses to Jesus. We point upward, beyond ourselves, to the One who deserves all glory and honor. Our message is the same—we are not the answer to our sin and brokenness; He is.

Pause and Reflect

1 Take a few minutes to consider that you were saved to be sent in a new direction.

2 How does thinking of ourselves as being sent reorient our lives around God's mission to seek and save the lost?

DISCUSSION QUESTIONS

1 What are some ideas people have about who God is and what He is like? How does Jesus fulfill and challenge our expectations of what God is like?

---

2 Based on the well-known phrase "word of God" in the Old Testament, why do you think John chose this title for Jesus? What is the relationship of "the Word" to God Himself?

---

3 What does it take to have confidence in someone? Given what John has told us about the Word, can you have confidence in Him? Why?

---

4 Do you know someone whose life reflects a belief in what John 1:1-5 says about Jesus? What stands out the most about such people?

---

5 Why did the divine Word—the Creator of all things, One with overcoming power—need a witness? What does this emphasis on a witness mean for us today?

---

6 What comes to mind when you think of "witnessing"? How does the example of John the Baptizer confirm or alter your view of being a witness?

---

7 Many find sharing their faith difficult and scary. In what ways does John the Baptizer's example clarify the subject of our witness? Is sharing the story of Jesus harder than giving your personal testimony? Why or why not?

---

8 Compare John 1:4-5 to 2 Corinthians 4:3-6. Can you feel the intensity of the spiritual battle? What can you do to display the light of Christ to the hearts of those around you?

---

9 When was the "but now" moment in your life? How was God's power evident in saving and changing you? How does your life before knowing Christ compare to your life now?

---

10 In what ways can our lives reflect the grace and truth of the gospel in our homes, our workplaces, and our extended families? How does our reflection of Christ's grace and truth help us bear witness to God's work?

Chapter 2

Jesus' Teaching

The Teaching of the Kingdom

matthew — parables re: Kingdom

Throughout history, defining events have shaped society and led to major changes in culture and the world. Often these changes have been credited to speeches given by eloquent and influential leaders.

We think of Martin Luther King Jr. and his "I Have a Dream" speech that captured the spirit behind the Civil Rights movement and ignited its supporters behind the cause for racial equality. We think of Ronald Reagan at the Berlin Wall in 1987 addressing the Soviet Union leader directly: "Mr. Gorbachev, tear down this wall!" Even though the national media didn't make much of the phrase at the time, historians today see it as a significant moment in the fall of Communism.

Of course, the monumental changes needed more than speeches. The Civil Rights movement needed the support and action of President Kennedy and federal legislators. Ronald Reagan's appeal depended on the response of Eastern Europe's powerful leaders. The words of these men gave voice to a vision, but multiple factors contributed to the eventual outcome.

The coming of God's kingdom in human history is different than these other events. There was no need for other people to ratify the vision and make it a reality. The kingdom came in one Man—Jesus—and with one message. His vision and His words were powerful because of who He is.

In this chapter, we will look at how the teaching ministry of Jesus Christ was centered on the kingdom of God—the arrival of God's reign in fulfillment of His promises to His people. The kingdom puts on display the saving power of God as it is proclaimed to all kinds of people. In response to Jesus' proclamation of the kingdom of God, we must repent of our own personal agendas, trust in Him as our King, and then represent Him faithfully in the world.

The kingdom has arrived with the coming of Jesus (Mark 1:14-15).

14 After John was arrested, Jesus went to Galilee, preaching the good news of God: 15 "The time is fulfilled, and the kingdom of God has come near. Repent and believe in the good news!"

The hope of a king was woven into the fabric of Israel's story. God's promise to Abraham to make him a great nation anticipated the need for a king (Gen. 12:1-3). In the law, God laid out the characteristics of a model king (Deut. 17:14-20). The Book of Judges revealed Israel's spiritual need for a king, for without one, the people did what was right in their own eyes (Judg. 21:25). The failed reign of King Saul taught Israel that his successor would have to be a man who followed God (1 Sam. 15:10). Throughout the Old Testament, we see kings come and go, each one pointing forward to the promised King who would bring hope and peace to the world.

But when Israel's promised King finally arrived on the scene, He surprised them. The Jewish people expected Him to come with majesty and power, to overthrow Rome and any other oppressors of Israel. They looked for a king like the one described in the Psalms: a king whose rule and reign extends over all things (Ps. 103:19), including the nations and kings of the earth (Ps. 47). They expected the establishment of God's kingdom to take place according to their preconceived ideas and their own timetable.

Instead, the King came quietly. He was born in a backwoods town called Bethlehem. He grew up as a carpenter's son in the village of Nazareth. But even if He did not come in the way His people thought He would, He *did* come to establish a kingdom. That's why we see Jesus in the passage above, at the start of His ministry, proclaiming the good news of God.

Put simply, the kingdom of God is the reign of God. There's nothing unusual about a Jewish prophet talking about God's kingdom. Prophets had long proclaimed that the Day of the Lord would come when God would return to His people and make everything right. What was unusual about Jesus' message was His declaration that the kingdom of God had come near.

You see, like all great leaders, Jesus fulfilled the hope of a people. He gathered followers. He confronted those who opposed Him. But unlike other great leaders, Jesus' greatness didn't depend on His success in these things. He is great because of who He is. Whereas other leaders are described as great because of what they accomplish, Jesus established His kingdom because of His innate greatness.

Martin Luther King Jr. had a dream, but the fulfillment of the dream was not in him. Ronald Reagan wanted the wall in Berlin torn down, but he had to appeal to someone else. The difference with Jesus was that when He said, "The kingdom of God has come near!" He was saying, "I am bringing it. It is in Me!" In other words, the achievement flowed from His greatness, not vice-versa. *That* is what shocked Jesus' hearers.

Because of Jesus, the kingdom is here now. It has arrived. But the full manifestation of the kingdom is not here yet. That's why Jesus told His followers to pray: Your kingdom come, Your will be done on earth as it is in heaven (Matt. 6:10). The kingdom is *already* and *not yet*. Both. At the same time. Already here because of Christ's first coming, but not yet here fully until Christ's second coming.

What should our response be to Jesus' message about the kingdom? Just what He said: repent and believe in the good news (Mark 1:15). The King calls for a response that requires self-denying sacrifice—admission of our sin and humble trust in Jesus the King.

The kingdom is the demonstration of God's saving power (Luke 4:16-21).

16 *He came to Nazareth, where He had been brought up. As usual, He entered the synagogue on the Sabbath day and stood up to read.* 17 *The scroll of the prophet Isaiah was given to Him, and unrolling the scroll, He found the place where it was written:*

18 *The Spirit of the Lord is on Me,*
because He has anointed Me
to preach good news to the poor.
He has sent Me
to proclaim freedom to the captives
and recovery of sight to the blind,
to set free the oppressed,
19 *to proclaim the year of the Lord's favor.*

20 *He then rolled up the scroll, gave it back to the attendant, and sat down. And the eyes of everyone in the synagogue were fixed on Him.* 21 *He began by saying to them, "Today as you listen, this Scripture has been fulfilled."*

In this passage, we get a glimpse of Jesus teaching in the synagogue (a Jewish place of worship) in Nazareth, the town where He grew up. According to the custom of the day, when His turn came, Jesus was supposed to stand and read from one of the prophets. He chose a passage from Isaiah that declared what the anointed king would do when he comes. Then He told everyone listening that Isaiah's words were being fulfilled right then and there. In other words, "This text is about Me and My ministry."

By choosing to read this portion of Isaiah, Jesus gave us a picture of His mission and of the power and presence of God's kingdom manifested on earth. The kingdom may be from heaven, but it directly affects things on earth.

What does the kingdom look like when it comes? It looks like a king who is preaching good news, healing the sick, and casting out demons. In other words, it looks like the pattern of Jesus' ministry that we find in Scripture.

In preaching the good news of the kingdom, Jesus was showing that salvation had to do with people being freed from captivity. When He healed people, Jesus was proving His power over the effects of the curse, that He is the King of kings and Lord of lords. When He restored sight to the blind, Jesus was declaring that in His kingdom, all things would be made right again.

People measure the greatness of earthly leaders by the effects they produce in the world and the changes that are implemented because of their influence. But the greatness of the God-anointed King is demonstrated in His power to transform the *hearts* of people! This passage contains the promise of transformed lives. The poor will receive His message as good news. The captive will be set free. The blind will see. The burdens of the oppressed will be lifted. Wherever we see Jesus ministering in the pages of the Gospels, we see Jesus fulfilling this vision.

Luke 4:16-21 was not a campaign platform. These words were far more than a vision statement for His ministry. They were not His strategic, long-term plan. Instead, this passage described the present reality of His ministry. God anointed Jesus as Messiah to do these things ("the Spirit of the Lord is upon Me"), and that's just what He did.

The Sermon on the Mount (Matt. 5–7) contains the basic teaching of Jesus to His people on what kingdom life looks like. The centerpiece of the sermon is the Lord's Prayer, and the center of the Lord's Prayer is the petition that God's kingdom come and His will be done on earth as it is in heaven.

But how do we know what life in God's kingdom looks like? Watch Jesus. Look at His ministry. See how His life and teaching were shaped by His identity as the promised King.

How do we know what the lives of God's kingdom people should look like? Watch the early church in Acts. There we are given a picture of what takes place when the Spirit of God empowers people to live according to Christ's kingdom mission. The people responded by repenting and believing. They joined with other believers in worshiping together, taking care of one another, and adding to their community through gospel proclamation.

The kingdom is proclaimed to all kinds of people (Luke 8:4-8).

4 *As a large crowd was gathering, and people were flocking to Him from every town, He said in a parable:* 5 *"A sower went out to sow his seed. As he was sowing, some fell along the path; it was trampled on, and the birds of the sky ate it up.* 6 *Other seed fell on the rock; when it sprang up, it withered, since it lacked moisture.* 7 *Other seed fell among thorns; the thorns sprang up with it and choked it.* 8 *Still other seed fell on good ground; when it sprang up, it produced a crop:* 100 *times what was sown." As He said this, He called out, "Anyone who has ears to hear should listen!"*

In His teaching, Jesus frequently made use of parables, stories related to everyday life that make a particular point. Many of Jesus' parables begin with the statement "The kingdom of God is like..." But this one does not. Perhaps this parable is less about what the kingdom *is like* and more about how the kingdom *begins.*

Notice that the story begins with a sower and seed. When Mark and Luke recount this parable, the seed is referred to as the Word of God (Mark 4:14; Luke 8:11). Matthew's telling connects the Word of God and the kingdom of God—the seed is the Word about the kingdom (Matt. 13:19). It is important to note that God uses His *Word* to produce kingdom fruit.

The parable is a story about the Word/seed being spread generously by the farmer but not being received by everyone. The fruitfulness of the seed depended on where it landed. Jesus said the seed fell in different places: on the path, on rocky ground, among thorns, or on good soil. On the path, the seed was trampled on and eaten by birds. The sun scorched the seeds that sprouted on the rocky ground since they lacked water. The seedlings among the thorns were choked out. But the good ground received the seed and produced fruit.

In the same way, when the Word of the kingdom comes into contact with receptive hearts, kingdom fruit is produced in people's lives. This fruit is evident when people use their lives as instruments of God's kingdom for the good of other people.

What does a receptive heart to the Word look like? James, the brother of Jesus, would later write about such a person who humbly receives the implanted Word, "who looks intently into the perfect law of freedom and perseveres in it, and is not a forgetful hearer but one who does good works—this person will be blessed in what he does" (Jas. 1:25). Do you see the contrast between the one who comes into contact with the Word but forgets (vv. 22-24) and the one who looks intently, whose life is shaped by the Word? The promise for the one who mediates on the Word and follows it is a blessed life.

The kingdom has authority because of the identity of the King (Matt. 7:28-29).

28 *When Jesus had finished this sermon, the crowds were astonished at His teaching,* 29 *because He was teaching them like one who had authority, and not like their scribes.*

Jesus' teaching took people by surprise. The crowds were amazed at two things: *the matter* and *the manner* of His teaching.

They were astounded by *what* He taught. He was different than anyone they had heard before. He didn't urge them to new forms of religion, to give more money, or to attend services more often. He didn't summon them to a greater commitment to a religious routine. He kept going back to their motives, to who they were deep inside. He said true religion wasn't a performance.

In the story that concluded Jesus' Sermon on the Mount, Jesus compared and contrasted two builders: one wise and one foolish (Matt. 7:24-27). His use of a building metaphor should not surprise us. Jesus was the son of a carpenter. He knew the difference between a solid house and a feeble one. But He was not giving construction lessons here; He was talking about building a life.

As you build your life, the foundation you choose shapes your life more than anything else. Jesus provided two options for building your life—either listen and receive His teaching or ignore His teaching.

The people were not only amazed at *what* Jesus taught but *how* He taught. His words struck the crowd. They realized that the manner in which Jesus taught communicated something about Himself. Jesus taught as one having authority, not as the teachers of the law.

Rabbis were highly educated. They knew 2,000 years of religious tradition inside and out. They had studied all the learned religious opinions, but they did not teach as if they had authority. They always appealed to the authority of religious tradition. The rabbis quoted the experts. Teaching from the rabbis was like listening to someone read an extended footnote. Jesus was different. He didn't use any footnotes. He was the final authority.

Consider how astonishing this must have been! Jesus was only 30 years old, which was not very old by the standards of the ancient world. He had grown up in Nazareth, a small town of little importance. He was a carpenter. He had not gone to the schools the rabbis attended. And yet Jesus spoke with an authority that exceeded that of the older scribes.

The prophets of the Old Testament did not speak with their own authority. They introduced their messages by saying, "Thus says the LORD." They spoke with the authority of God. But Jesus *never* used that phrase. He spoke with His own authority when He interpreted or reapplied the law, when He made promises, when He commanded, and when He prohibited. The people had never heard anyone do that before.

Unfortunately, most of the people who heard Jesus did not bring their lives in line with His teaching. They were merely impressed. Amazed, but not changed.

Too many times, we stop at just being impressed with Jesus' words. Religious leaders, professors, literary writers, and moral people all over the world have long been impressed with Jesus' teaching. But this isn't enough. In order to receive kingdom teaching and experience kingdom fruit, we must receive Jesus' teaching with repentance and belief.

Conclusion

Jesus wants us to recognize His authority, but more importantly, He wants us to respond to His teaching in faith, believing His kingdom is true and that His instruction is for our good. It's only in trusting that Jesus' kingdom is true and relevant in all areas of life that we will begin living in light of the astonishing authority of King Jesus.

What does this life under the rule of King Jesus look like? It looks like the life of our King—a life of love that gives itself for others. When Jesus announced that the kingdom of God was near, He was referring to His presence. The arrival of God's kingdom means the sending out of His ambassadors. The kingdom has come, so now we are to go. Ed Stetzer writes: "As believers, we move forward in missional ministry as ambassadors of the King who travels with us by the Holy Spirit."[3]

- -

Voices from *the Church*

"God's Word, working through God's Spirit, is God's primary instrument for growing God's church."[4]
–Jonathan Leeman

- -

Voices from *Church History*

"He is truly the Sower of all that is good, and we are his farm. The whole harvest of spiritual fruits is by him and from him."[5]
–Cyril of Alexandria (circa 376-444)

Devotions

KING OF WISDOM

Can you remember the last time you had to make a decision and didn't know what to do? What about the last time someone asked you for advice and you didn't have an answer? These moments can be confusing and unsettling. Thankfully, most of the time, they pass pretty quickly. Things get figured out. But have you ever thought about what it would be like if these moments never got resolved? What would it be like if we lived in world with no answers, no guidance, no wisdom?

This kind of world is hard for us to imagine. But God could envision a world with absolutely no wisdom in it. He knew that a world filled with people doing what is right in their own eyes would destroy His creation. There would be no peace. People would not prosper. Everyone would live in confusion all the time.

Take a moment to read Deuteronomy 17:18-19, where God provided a way for wise counsel to be available to His people. He said, in effect, "My Word will be written down, and the leader of My people will know My Word. Because My Word will shape his life, he will be strong, his ways will prosper, and God will be with him.

The problem for the nation of Israel was that their history was filled with kings unlike the one described in Deuteronomy 17. But Jesus is this type of king.

An early sign that He was the model King was when He was 12 years old and He entered the synagogue and taught the religious leaders. Another sign was when He entered the wilderness and faced temptation as One who had taken counsel from the Word. Then He taught with clarity and authority, demonstrating keen awareness of the hearts of people and the Word of God. This is the reason Paul called Him the wisdom of God (Col. 2:3).

Pause and Reflect

1 Where do you seek wisdom?

---

2 How should you respond to the revelation that Jesus is the wisdom of God?

KING OF GLORY

Psalm 24:7-8: "Lift up your heads, you gates! Rise up, ancient doors! Then the King of glory will come in. Who is this King of glory?"

Waiting for something we want desperately can be difficult. But there's also a sense of excitement and hopefulness in waiting. Anticipation makes us more alert to what is happening around us. When we sit somewhere and wait for a friend, we continually look up and around to see if they are coming. We may even think we spot them before they arrive. It is hard to focus on anything else.

It's good for us to be reminded that we are waiting for something. Israel's history had celebrations and rituals intended to remind them they were waiting for a king. One such moment is described in Psalm 24.

In the midst of this public drama of celebration, there is a powerful give and take between the people of God and the priest. The priest would call out to lift up the city gates so the "King of glory" could enter in. The people responded with the question "Who is this King of glory?"

This question remains relevant even today. "Who is this King of glory?" The New Testament reveals that He is Jesus (Mark 1:14-15). That's why as we look to the life of Jesus, we should *remember* His coming and His establishing the kingdom of God even as we *wait* for His return.

Pause and Reflect

1   Do you remember the last time you waited for something? Describe that experience.

----

2   What does God want us to remember now, even as we wait?

KINGDOM MISSION

Imagine you are standing in the Galilean crowd when Jesus announced that the kingdom of God had come near. As you look straight at Him, you hear the collective gasp from those standing around you. Your eyes don't shift. Time seems to be standing still.

In slow motion, it seems, He stops talking, and He walks away from the crowd. You know He is calling for a response. And one thought is swirling in your mind—*He has just declared Himself to be a King with a kingdom, but the kingdom is not visible. So what will He do to build it?*

What He does next makes no sense, and yet it makes all the sense in the world. He approaches a group of fishermen on the seashore and calls them to follow Him. He does not build His kingdom with soldiers but fishermen. He tells the fishermen to leave their nets, for they are going to catch people. As they follow, He begins to teach them what it means to catch people and to teach them to follow Him. Jesus casts out evil spirits, heals the sick, and preaches the good news. Jesus gathers followers who will join Him in this kingdom mission.

Then it hits you. Time is no longer moving in slow motion. You are now faced with the question—Will I follow this One who speaks with authority and who is gathering people for a kingdom that is here even if I can't see it completely? Can I give what it will cost personally? Will I respond with ongoing repentance and faith? Am I willing to join Him in the kingdom-building mission?

Pause and Reflect

1   What is one thing you must give up to follow Jesus' kingdom mission?

---

2   What changes in your life do you need to make in order to be a part of this mission?

Discussion Questions

1   What do you think of when you hear the phrase "the kingdom of God"? How does Jesus use this term? Why do you think Jesus speaks of the kingdom's arrival as good news?

2   In what ways does Jesus' announcement call for us to trade our personal kingdom agendas for Christ's kingdom agenda? Why is it important that repentance and faith are seen as more than a one-time event?

3   How many great achievements would you be able to accomplish without the help of anyone else? How does our need for others compare with the innate authority and power of Jesus to cast a vision and fulfill it Himself?

4   In what ways should our lives demonstrate the saving power of God's kingdom? How is Christ's authority demonstrated in our witness as His people?

5   In what ways can we enjoy life under King Jesus when it is clear we are still living in a broken world? How does the church point forward to the day when the kingdom will come in its fullness?

6   How does the phrase "the Word about the kingdom" help you more fully understand the story line and the purpose of Scripture? In what ways are you actively "sowing the seed" of the gospel?

7   What are some practical ways for a Christian to look intently into the Word? What is the role of faith in our encounter with the Word?

8   How does the stark contrast between the builders in Matthew 7 influence our witness toward friends and family members who have not built their lives on the foundation of Christ's kingdom?

9   What are some ways we as Christians fall short of living under Jesus' authority and are merely impressed with His teaching?

10   How do you live your life in such a way that the kingdom agenda of God's mission is obvious?

Chapter 3

Jesus' Miracles

The Power of the Kingdom

"He comes to make His blessings flow Far as the curse is found." This we affirm every year as we celebrate and sing Christmas hymns. This beautiful lyric from "Joy to the World" looks ahead to Christ's promised return while giving us a glimpse of what Jesus did when He first came to earth.

Previously we saw that the primary message of Christ's teaching concerned the kingdom—the reign of God. Jesus declared that the kingdom had come, and He taught through His words that He Himself was God's promised King. The long-awaited King and kingdom had arrived for the people of God.

Of course, it's one thing to *say* that the kingdom had arrived. It's another thing to *show* the kingdom's power. Jesus did both. He proclaimed in word *and* deed that the blessings of God would flow "far as the curse is found," reaching into every nook and cranny of our world and turning back the terrible effects of our sin.

In this chapter, we will see how through signs and wonders Jesus demonstrated the truth of His proclamation that God's kingdom was coming through His ministry. Jesus' miracles put on display the compassion of God for human beings held captive by the effects of the curse that resulted from our sin. Because of Christ's power to save and restore, we are no longer enslaved to sin, and we are freed by the King to live for His kingdom.

Jesus' miracles signified His compassion for people (Mark 1:29-34).

29 *As soon as they left the synagogue, they went into Simon and Andrew's house with James and John.* 30 *Simon's mother-in-law was lying in bed with a fever, and they told Him about her at once.* 31 *So He went to her, took her by the hand, and raised her up. The fever left her, and she began to serve them.*

32 *When evening came, after the sun had set, they began bringing to Him all those who were sick and those who were demon-possessed.* 33 *The whole town was assembled at the door,* 34 *and He healed many who were sick with various diseases and drove out many demons. But He would not permit the demons to speak, because they knew Him.*

Jesus felt for people. He wasn't a stoic leader floating through the world doing good out of obligation or formality. The Gospels tell us He was "moved with compassion." This phrase shines light on what motivated Jesus to heal the sick, cast out demons, and give sight to the blind. When He encountered those suffering from diseases, demon possession, and hunger,

He was moved with compassion to alleviate their suffering (Matt. 14:14; 15:32; 20:34; Mark 1:41; 5:19; Luke 7:13-14). When He considered His people—the weary and scattered "sheep without a shepherd"—He was moved with compassion to lead them as God's anointed King (Matt. 9:36).

We see the compassion of Jesus on full display in the story about Simon Peter's mother-in-law. Just moments after Jesus entered the house, He found out Simon's mother-in-law was ill. He went to her side, touched her, and healed her. Later, after the sun set, Jesus continued to show compassion for those suffering by healing the sick and driving out demons from those brought to Him.

This passage draws our attention to the comprehensive power of Jesus and His kingdom. We see that His healing powers reigned over both sickness and the demonic, over both the physical and spiritual ailments that distort God's good creation and reflect the Evil One's power in this fallen world.

Sickness reveals the brokenness and deteriorating effects of the fall on creation. Eyes that were designed to see are closed off to light and unable to recognize objects (Mark 10:46-52). Ears that were made to hear are unable to receive sound (7:31-37). Legs that were made to walk are folded under the body (John 5:1-15). People are so sick that they are unable to get up from their bed (Mark 6:53-56).

Demon possession reveals that there is a personal enemy with an army in our world, one who has a hold on people's hearts and minds. Jesus showed compassion to those controlled by demonic spirits. He demonstrated His sovereign power over those forces by casting them out of the people who were possessed (Mark 5:1-20).

This is the world Jesus came to—a world broken by sin, languishing under the effects of the fall, populated with people enslaved to evil desires. But through Jesus' ministry, we see that the present world is not the way it is supposed to be. When God takes charge, things are different. When His kingdom comes, the world is changed. The effects of the fall are reversed in the light of King Jesus.

Once Christ delivers us from bondage to sin and Satan, we are free! That's why Simon's mother-in-law is an example for us. Once she was healed, she immediately began to serve. Service follows salvation. This is God's grand design. He saves us from sin and death to service and worship.

It's a pattern we see elsewhere in Scripture:

- In Exodus 3:10-12, God sent Moses to lead Israel out of slavery in order that they might be free to worship God.
- In John 9, Jesus healed a man who had been blind from birth. At the end of the account (vv. 30-33), the once-blind man now sees, and we find him worshiping God and telling others about what Jesus did for him.
- In 2 Corinthians 5:14-15, we see that understanding the gospel message leads us to no longer live for ourselves but for Him who loves us and gave His life for us.
- In Romans 12:1-2, Paul exhorts us on the basis of God's great mercy to live our lives for God.
- In Ephesians 1:3-14, Paul said that God saves us so we will praise Him.

Do you see the pattern? We are saved to worship and serve. Service and worship flow out of the hearts of the redeemed.

Jesus' miracles signified His power and authority (John 6:1-14).

1 *After this, Jesus crossed the Sea of Galilee (or Tiberias).* 2 *And a huge crowd was following Him because they saw the signs that He was performing by healing the sick.* 3 *So Jesus went up a mountain and sat down there with His disciples.*

4 *Now the Passover, a Jewish festival, was near.* 5 *Therefore, when Jesus looked up and noticed a huge crowd coming toward Him, He asked Philip, "Where will we buy bread so these people can eat?"* 6 *He asked this to test him, for He Himself knew what He was going to do.*

7 *Philip answered, "Two hundred denarii worth of bread wouldn't be enough for each of them to have a little."*

8 *One of His disciples, Andrew, Simon Peter's brother, said to Him,* 9 *"There's a boy here who has five barley loaves and two fish—but what are they for so many?"*

10 *Then Jesus said, "Have the people sit down."*

There was plenty of grass in that place, so they sat down. The men numbered about 5,000. 11 *Then Jesus took the loaves, and after giving thanks He distributed them to those who were seated—so also with the fish, as much as they wanted.*

12 *When they were full, He told His disciples, "Collect the leftovers so that nothing is wasted."* 13 *So they collected them and filled 12 baskets with the pieces from the five barley loaves that were left over by those who had eaten.*

14 *When the people saw the sign He had done, they said, "This really is the Prophet who was to come into the world!"*

Did you notice the interaction between Jesus and His disciples? It began with Jesus asking Philip, "How will we feed all these people?" Jesus asked this question, John tells us, in order to test Philip. The test was this: "Whose power and authority will you trust?"

It's the kind of test we encounter every time we face a situation that seems outside of our control. Will we trust in our own strength or will we look to the One who has all power? In this passage, Philip admitted the disciples' weakness: "There is not enough money to buy supper for everyone." Then Andrew brought a boy forward who had five pieces of bread and two fish. Unfortunately, not even Andrew could fathom that Jesus would use such a small meal to feed everyone. He shrugged ("What are they for so many?") and joined Philip in thinking they had nothing to offer the people.

But Jesus took what Andrew found and instructed everyone to sit down. And multiplying the fish and bread, he communicated through this sign, "I have something to feed them." Jesus fed the crowd until they were full.

In this story, Jesus was doing much more than merely feeding people. He was demonstrating His own power and authority in a way that shined light on His identity. Remember the Old Testament account of Moses leading the people of Israel through the wilderness? God provided manna from heaven in order to sustain His people.

Here Jesus had miraculously fed five thousand people in the wilderness. He was the new Moses who was ready to lead a new exodus (out of slavery to sin) for a new Israel. Just as Israel was sustained by bread from heaven, Jesus' followers are sustained by the Bread of heaven—Jesus Himself.

Unfortunately, as the story goes on, we see that the people didn't understand the sign. They misinterpreted Jesus' identity. They wanted His power but without His authority. So after they rightly declared Him to be "the Prophet," Jesus left them because the crowd was about to "take Him by force to make Him king" (John 6:14-15). And the kind of king they envisioned was not the kind of king Jesus was—the King who would give His life for His people.

So why were the people following Him? Because of the signs Jesus performed. Their interest in Him was motivated by the desire to encounter more of the benefits of His power. Earlier in John's Gospel, we see people responding to Jesus because of His miraculous works: "Jesus, however, would not entrust Himself to them, since He knew them all" (John 2:23-24). Jesus knew that something was wrong with their intentions. He knew their hearts. He knew their enthusiasm was not about Him but about what He could do for them.

This problem is present in our day as well. Sometimes people have great enthusiasm for Jesus, but the Jesus they are excited about is not the real, biblical Jesus. They are excited about a Jesus of their own imagination—one who will fulfill their existing aspirations, hopes, and dreams instead of the biblical Jesus who gives us new aspirations, hopes, and dreams. Too often we misunderstand what it means for Jesus to be King.

Jesus invites us to see His glory through the pages of Scripture, but not so we might get excited about how useful His power is in getting what we want. Rather, He wants us to know Him as King, to place our trust in Him and in the promises that He has made to us.

Jesus' miracles signified His identity as the promised Messiah (Luke 7:18-23).

18 *Then John's disciples told him about all these things. So John summoned two of his disciples* 19 *and sent them to the Lord, asking, "Are You the One who is to come, or should we look for someone else?"*

20 *When the men reached Him, they said, "John the Baptist sent us to ask You, 'Are You the One who is to come, or should we look for someone else?'"*

21 *At that time Jesus healed many people of diseases, plagues, and evil spirits, and He granted sight to many blind people.* 22 *He replied to them, "Go and report to John the things you have seen and heard: The blind receive their sight, the lame walk, those with skin diseases are healed, the deaf hear, the dead are raised, and the poor are told the good news.* 23 *And anyone who is not offended because of Me is blessed."*

Questions raise the stakes in conversations. When someone asks you a question, it puts you on the spot. If a question is not directed to you but you are within earshot of it, you likely lean in to hear how the person will respond.

As we look to John the Baptizer's question, it is important to understand what he was actually asking. John was not openly questioning God, and he was not questioning whether the Messiah would come. Instead, John was asking Jesus if He was the Messiah. The question is particularly intriguing in light of his previous proclamation that Jesus is the Messiah, the Lamb of God who takes away the sin of the world (John 1:29,32-34).

What was John up to? It seems he had a very specific vision of what the Messiah would be like. Put in the most pointed way, John was saying to Jesus, "Remove the doubt! Tell us if You are the One we've been waiting for!"

Jesus did not answer John directly. His response was very simple. He told John's disciples to report back what they had witnessed (Luke 7:22). Through this response, Jesus told John to consider what the Scriptures say about the Messiah, to compare the prophecies of the Old Testament with His deeds and teaching. What Jesus was implying was that His works spoke for themselves. They were the sign that Jesus was truly the Messiah.

Our circumstances often affect how confidently we trust Jesus. It is easy for us to wonder why things are not happening the way we expect. This can lead us to one of three spiritual dangers.

First, we may be tempted to question the truthfulness of what we believe. When we do this, we allow our circumstances and our expectations of what is supposed to happen to have more authority than what God has promised us in His Word.

Second, we may be tempted to believe that God is treating us unfairly. We forget to trust in God's sovereign goodness for us (Rom. 8:28). It is a challenge in difficult times to remember that God is molding us into the image of Jesus Christ and wants to use us in the lives of other people. Sometimes we have to face hardships and challenges in order for us to be in the place where God wants to use us.

Third, we may be tempted to believe that God is punishing us for something we have done in the past. While it is true that God uses the consequences of bad decisions to discipline us and train us, God does not punish those who have saving faith in Jesus (Rom. 8:1). When we believe that God is punishing us, we begin to look for ways to please God so that the punishment stops and He will bless us again. This idea causes us to think that our good behavior earns from God good days and good circumstances. But this undermines our relationship with Him, which is built on grace and faith in His promises to us.

Life under the sovereign authority of a benevolent King navigates these three temptations by trusting in the identity, power, authority, and goodness of King Jesus. Our Savior does not fit into the boxes of earthly expectations we would put Him in. Like John the Baptizer, we should look at what Jesus said and what Jesus did and then center our vision of God on Him, not our preconceived notions.

Conclusion

Jesus wants us to become convinced of His identity as Messiah so that we freely live for Him under His loving reign. It's in trusting that Jesus is the true King that we find faith, hope, and love. We want our lives to be characterized by service and worship totally dependent upon Him as the Bread from heaven in the midst of any circumstance that we face.

What does this life under the rule of King Jesus look like? It is a life where we are free—free from fear, doubt, and worry and free to worship the one true God and to join Him on mission.

HYMN OF *Response*

"At the name of Jesus, Ev'ry knee shall bow,
Ev'ry tongue confess Him King of glory now;
'Tis the Father's pleasure We should call Him Lord,
Who from the beginning Was the mighty Word.

Humbled for a season, To receive a name
From the lips of sinners Unto whom He came,
Faithfully He bore it, Spotless to the last,
Brought it back victorious When from death He passed.

In your hearts enthrone Him; There let Him subdue
All that is not holy, All that is not true;
Crown Him as your captain In temptation's hour;
Let His will enfold you In its light and power.

Watch, for this Lord Jesus Shall return again,
With His Father's glory O'er the earth to reign;
For the day is coming When each knee shall bow,
So let hearts confess Him King of glory now."
–Caroline M. Noel

Devotions

CRUMBLING FROM THE INSIDE

Isaiah 54:10: "Though the mountains move and the hills shake, My love will not be removed from you and My covenant of peace will not be shaken,' says your compassionate LORD."

All around our house, we have rock walls that are over 40 years old. Recently, we've had do some maintenance on them. We could see some weak places in the walls, and we were concerned that they may not hold up much longer. One small section needed just a little cosmetic work. But as we started working on it, we discovered the rocks inside the wall were literally crumbling.

Our lives are a lot like these walls. There are places where we show strain from the pressure we are under. Quick-tempered. Compulsive decisions. Paralyzing anxiety. There are also places where we are crumbling from the inside. Hidden addiction. Self-protective confidence. Persistent temptation to doubt. In either case, it seems that if one thing shifts or if one more thing is put on our load, we will cave in.

The God of compassion reminds us in Isaiah 54:10 that our foundation is not established on our own strength but on His love. Though the terrain around our lives moves, God says you will not be undone, for the One who created the mountains and the hills will remain faithful to us. He says, "I will make your fortifications out of rubies, your gates out of sparkling stones, and all your walls out of precious stones...you will be established on a foundation of righteousness" (vv. 12,14).

Pause and Reflect

1   Consider the places in your life where the pressure is the greatest. What do you fear? What causes you to be despondent? What do you feel like you have to control?

- -

2   Read 1 Peter 2:6. Give thanks to Jesus for being the sufficient foundation for your life, and express faith that in Him you will never be put to shame.

Signs and Satisfaction

Good memories, beauty, and pleasure are all great things, but they don't satisfy us in all times and in all situations. We can spend a lot of time, money, energy, and emotions to recover past experiences, capture the beauty that we desire, fulfill the longing of our dreams, and satisfy our search for pleasure. Isaiah described all of this as "spend[ing] money on what is not food" (55:2).

The truth is these things are not what we most deeply desire anyway. How do we know this? Because they don't satisfy us. Those things are, in C. S. Lewis' words, "the scent of a flower we have not found, the echo of a tune we have not heard, news from a country we have never yet visited."[3]

A tempting place to look for "the flower" is in religious activities. We are attracted to the confidence we see in people of faith, and we are inspired to try to increase ours. We leave church with a good feeling, and we commit to go more often. We think positively after reading our Bible and praying, and we declare our intentions to read and pray daily.

Jesus reminds us that there is a danger in religious activity at the expense of a relationship with God. Looking at a large crowd gathered around Him, He said, "You are looking for Me, not because you saw the signs, but because you ate the loaves and were filled" (John 6:26). These people He sent away. Why? Because all they wanted was to be filled again. What Jesus wants is for us to know Him as the Messiah, for He knows that He alone will satisfy us.

Pause and Reflect

1   What are some things that you have desired but have really never satisfied you?

- -

2   Take a moment to confess ways you have tried to use Jesus to get what you want; then express your confidence in His reign over your life.

Restored for Mission

Mark 10:52: "'Go your way,' Jesus told him. 'Your faith has healed you.' Immediately he could see and began to follow Him on the road."

Have you ever been really sick? Maybe even suffered from a lifelong illness or handicap like Bartimaeus, who was blind?

We know from Scripture that illness and death were not a part of God's original plan for His creation. We weren't made to be blind. We were made to see. We weren't made to suffer chronic pain, endure debilitating health problems, and fight persistent thoughts of depression. We were made to live and flourish under God's goodness and glory and to spread His goodness over the entire world.

Thankfully, this is still God's hope for us today. That's why His plan centers on the coming of a Savior who would inaugurate the kingdom of God on earth and push back the ill-effects of the fall. Isaiah 35:5 tells us one of the signs of the coming of the kingdom of God is that "the eyes of the blind will be opened." In Mark 10, we see the effects of the fall on Bartimaeus reversed. Jesus asked Him what he wanted. He replied confidently, "I want to see." And Jesus healed him.

Bartimaeus was restored with sight, and he was also restored to the mission for which he was made—to spread the glory of God to all people. When he experienced the power of the kingdom, he did not skip a beat. Mark tells us that he "immediately" joined Jesus in His mission. His response to the miraculous power of Christ was to follow Him. His restored sight led to service and worship.

Pause and Reflect

1   If Jesus asked you today, "What do you want?" what would you say?

2   If Jesus said to you today, "Follow Me," what would you do?

3   In response to God's saving work in your life, what is one way you will join Jesus' mission today?

DISCUSSION QUESTIONS

1   What would life today be like if everything were suddenly the way God intended it to be? What are some of the most common effects of the fall in our world today?

2   How does Christ's work reverse the effects of the fall? What are some tangible ways you see these physical and spiritual effects being reversed by Christ's work through His people?

3   How does your life reflect the compassion of Jesus? In what ways has the compassion of Christ been made known to you through Jesus' followers? How can we ensure that Christ's compassionate heart is our motivation for telling others about Jesus and doing other good deeds?

4   Why is worship and service the natural response to salvation? How do our actions demonstrate the arrival of the kingdom in our world?

5   If Jesus already knew He was going to perform a miracle, why did He ask the disciples about buying bread? What do the disciples' answers reveal about their faith? How do tests like this expose the tendencies of our own hearts? Why do you think we often have a difficult time believing in Christ's ability to change anything in our life?

6   What is the difference between being a consumer and being a worshiper? How can recognizing this difference shape your relationship with Jesus?

7   Has there been a time in your life when God shattered your expectations? How should we deal with disillusionment when God's plan does not work according to our own? How would you help a disillusioned Christian through a time of questioning God's goodness?

8   Questioning God's truthfulness, God's fairness, or God's grace—which of these three temptations do you encounter most often? What are some promises of Jesus that can strengthen our faith to resist these thoughts?

9   What does it look like to be an ambassador for the kingdom of God? How can Christ's powerful demonstration of the kingdom give us confidence in proclaiming the gospel?

Chapter 4

The Cross

The King's Identity as Suffering Messiah

North by Northwest, a classic Alfred Hitchcock movie, is a tale of mistaken identity. Throughout the film, agents of a mysterious organization pursue an innocent man across the United States, assuming he is someone else. Because of one inopportune moment that takes place in a hotel lobby, the innocent man is mistaken for someone else, and the stage is set for a thrilling turn of events.

Previously we've looked at the message Jesus taught (the kingdom of God has come) and the way He demonstrated the truth of His teaching (through miracles and signs). Crowds of people came to see Him. Jesus was a hot topic of conversation—something of a first-century celebrity. It's no surprise that many rumors and speculations were circulating about Him.

Because of His message and work, many came to the conclusion that He was the Messiah they had been waiting for. They were right about His identity but wrong about what that identity really meant. It wasn't so much a case of mistaken identity (as in *North by Northwest*) as it was a case of misunderstanding the *nature* of His identity.

In this chapter we see Jesus revealing to His disciples that He was indeed the long-awaited Messiah who would suffer for His people. Though His disciples didn't understand the idea of a Messiah who suffered, Jesus linked His suffering with His mission. On the night before His death, He spoke of Himself as the fulfillment of the Old Testament promises. The next day, Jesus was crucified in Jerusalem, where He gave up His life and took upon Himself the punishment that we deserve for our rebellion against God. God's kingdom comes through redemptive suffering.

Jesus is the Messiah-King who suffers for His people (Matt. 16:13-16,21-24).

13 *When Jesus came to the region of Caesarea Philippi, He asked His disciples, "Who do people say that the Son of Man is?"*

14 *And they said, "Some say John the Baptist; others, Elijah; still others, Jeremiah or one of the prophets."*

15 *"But you," He asked them, "who do you say that I am?"*

16 *Simon Peter answered, "You are the Messiah, the Son of the living God!"*

21 *From then on Jesus began to point out to His disciples that He must go to Jerusalem and suffer many things from the elders, chief priests, and scribes, be killed, and be raised the third day.* 22 *Then Peter took Him aside and began to rebuke Him, "Oh no, Lord! This will never happen to You!"*

23 *But He turned and told Peter, "Get behind Me, Satan! You are an offense to Me because you're not thinking about God's concerns, but man's."*

24 *Then Jesus said to His disciples, "If anyone wants to come with Me, he must deny himself, take up his cross, and follow Me.*

The setting of a story matters. It not only gives you a picture of the place where the story happened, it also helps you envision the events, connect with the characters involved, and understand the story's significance.

In Matthew 16:13-28, we witness one of the most important conversations Jesus had with His disciples. And the setting (Caesarea Philippi) served to intensify the moment. This place had a well-known temple to Caesar and a shrine to one of the gods. It was here that Jesus affirmed the announcement that He was the King whom God had promised to send to Israel, the Messiah who would rule the whole world (Ps. 2:8). What a setting for such an announcement!

Jesus' first question to His disciples was general and impersonal: "Who do *people* say that *the Son of Man* is?" The disciples mentioned the rumors: "You are a prophet like Jeremiah, a miracle-worker like Elijah, or John the Baptist."

Jesus' second question was direct and personal: "Who do *you* say that *I am*?" Peter spoke first, announcing, "You are the Messiah, the Son of the living God!" With this, Peter confessed that Jesus is the anointed King whom God promised to Israel. As the Son, Jesus is the rightful Heir of God's kingdom (2 Sam. 7:14; Ps. 2:7).

Peter got the answer right. Even more, Jesus said that God revealed the answer to Peter. But it quickly became clear that he didn't understand all his answer entailed. Merely stating that Jesus is the Messiah is not enough. We must also know why He came and how He planned to accomplish His mission. In addition to recognizing the Messiah, we also must accept the mission of the Messiah.

Jesus then took the conversation in a new direction: "*From then on* Jesus began to point out…" At this point, Jesus concluded His Galilean ministry and began His journey toward Jerusalem. From Caesarea Philippi, Jesus began to teach that whatever would happen to Him *must* happen. He traveled in the direction of Jerusalem with a sense of determination (see Mark 10:32-34).

After Jesus revealed that He was the Messiah who would suffer for His people, Peter's true but limited understanding of the Messiah's mission was put on display. Peter rebuked Jesus for saying He must die. In response to this, Jesus said two things: First, if you stand in the way of His suffering, you are standing in the way of His identity and mission (Matt. 16:23). Second, once you confess His identity, you are joining Him in mission (v. 24).

Acknowledging Jesus as Messiah has major implications for our lives. First, we must remember that we are confessing Him as King. He has the prerogative to declare what kind of King He is and how He will accomplish His purposes. It is His authority, not ours. Acknowledging Jesus as King means we will follow His lead and offer Him full loyalty and devotion.

Second, we must remember that the gospel message is incomplete without the cross. Recognizing Jesus as the Messiah was a good first step, but it was not sufficient when the disciples' concept of Jesus as the Messiah differed so greatly from His own. It is not enough to confess that Jesus is the Messiah (16:16) if we do not also understand that His mission involves suffering and death (vv. 21-23).

Third, if Jesus' mission involved the cross, then those who would follow Him must embrace the same. We are called to take up our cross and follow Him (v. 24). We are called to lose our lives for Him in exchange for life everlasting (v. 25).

Jesus is the sacrificial Lamb who brings about the new covenant (Matt. 26:26-29).

26 *As they were eating, Jesus took bread, blessed and broke it, gave it to the disciples, and said, "Take and eat it; this is My body." 27 Then He took a cup, and after giving thanks, He gave it to them and said, "Drink from it, all of you. 28 For this is My blood that establishes the covenant; it is shed for many for the forgiveness of sins. 29 But I tell you, from this moment I will not drink of this fruit of the vine until that day when I drink it in a new way in My Father's kingdom with you."*

Think about the meals we share together. We never gather *just* to eat but also to share time at the table. We celebrate birthdays, holidays, and special occasions, usually by sharing a meal. These moments at the table communicate something about an event's importance, and they connect us to each other in a way that other activities do not. So it's no surprise that on the night before His death, Jesus chose to explain the significance of His suffering with a meal.

God had established the Passover meal in order to remind His people of how He released them from slavery in Egypt. After nine different plagues, Pharaoh remained hardened to the idea of releasing the Israelites to go and worship their God. So God sent Moses to Pharaoh one last time to warn him of the tenth plague: the death of all the firstborn sons in Egypt.

In preparation for their escape from Egypt, God laid out steps for the Israelites to express their faith. They were instructed to take an unblemished lamb or goat into their home for four days. Then they were to kill the animal at twilight, spread its blood on the doorpost, and eat the meat that night. Moses told the Israelites that as the Lord executed the tenth plague in the land of Egypt, He would pass over all the households that put their faith in Him by honoring the Passover. The sign of faith would be the blood of the unblemished lamb smeared on the doorposts.

More than a thousand years later, Jesus used the Passover as the setting for His final meal with His disciples. Jesus not only proclaimed that He was the Messiah who would suffer, but He also explained the purpose of His death. He was suffering the punishment due His people. Jesus entered Israel's most celebrated story and showed how it pointed forward to Him.

Jesus took the Passover meal and demonstrated to His disciples how the promises of God's covenant with His people are fulfilled in Him. Taking the bread and the wine, He redirected His disciples' attention from the past to Himself, essentially saying, "The event we look to and celebrate is actually fulfilled in Me!" In breaking the bread and declaring that it is His body and in holding up the cup and declaring that it is His blood, He proclaimed His identity as the ultimate Passover Lamb who "takes away the sin of the world" (John 1:29).

But Jesus not only pointed back to the old covenant. He also pointed forward to the new covenant God had promised through the prophet Jeremiah: "I will be your God, and you will be My people" (see Jer. 31:33). Israel's history was moving forward to this moment when the new covenant would become a reality.

After they were released from Egypt and led through the wilderness for 40 years, Israel finally arrived in the promised land. But because of their disobedience and unfaithfulness to the law, God disciplined them and ultimately led them out of His land and into exile. Years later, God's grace made a way for them to return to the land and rebuild the temple and the walls of Jerusalem. Nevertheless, even after this return, the people's hearts were not changed.

Moses (Deut. 30:6) and Jeremiah (Jer. 31:33) had spoken of a day to come in which a process of transformation would take place in the hearts of God's people. The old covenant celebrated the work God did *for* His people, but the new covenant celebrated His work *in* them.

In Jeremiah 31, quoted in Hebrews 8, God promised that He would establish a new covenant with His people. God promised that He would give His people new hearts.

The glory of the new covenant can be demonstrated with three observations:
1. God will write His law on the hearts of His people, and they will love, depend on, and obey Him (Heb. 8:10a; compare to v. 9).
2. God does not make a conditional promise in the new covenant. He speaks definitively about His relationship with His people (v. 10b; compare to v. 9).
3. God promises to be merciful toward His people and not to hold their sins against them (v. 12, compare to v. 9).

For these reasons, Hebrews 8:6 describes the new covenant with "better promises."

During the last supper, Jesus said He was establishing the new covenant. No longer would we be bound to laws etched in stone. Instead, God would write His law on our hearts, and we would love Him, depend on Him, and obey Him out of gratitude. No longer would our sins come between us and God. Instead, God would shower us with His mercy and never hold our sins against us. All of this would take place through the death of Jesus—the Passover Lamb.

Jesus is the self-giving King who brings salvation to His people (Matt. 27:45-50).

45 *From noon until three in the afternoon darkness came over the whole land.* 46 *About three in the afternoon Jesus cried out with a loud voice, "Elí, Elí, lemá sabachtháni?" that is, "My God, My God, why have You forsaken Me?"*

47 *When some of those standing there heard this, they said, "He's calling for Elijah!"*

48 *Immediately one of them ran and got a sponge, filled it with sour wine, fixed it on a reed, and offered Him a drink.* 49 *But the rest said, "Let's see if Elijah comes to save Him!"*

50 *Jesus shouted again with a loud voice and gave up His spirit.*

The setting of Jesus' conversation with His disciples at Caesarea Philippi was significant. In front of the grand sites for pagan worship, Jesus affirmed that He was the Messiah sent to rule over the whole world (Ps. 2:4-9).

Now, in this passage that describes Jesus' sacrifice, we discover again how the setting helps us understand the story's message. Matthew records how darkness came over the whole land from noon until three in the afternoon. It was midday, and it was dark at the time the sun usually shines brightest.

It must have been an ominous moment, right? Something unmistakable was occurring. Everyone present must have had a clear sense that it was not supposed to be this way. As God's judgment for sin came down upon His innocent Son, even the weather was affected.

Those standing at the foot of the cross may have seen the darkness as God's judgment upon Israel for rejecting the Messiah. Perhaps they saw it as a sign that this crucifixion was unjust. Because of human sin, even the earth groans under the weight of corruption (Rom. 8:19-22). But in the midst of this political, social, and physical darkness, God's redemptive plan went forward, and His only Son—the Light of the world—took upon Himself all the darkness of divine judgment for our sin.

Then Jesus cried out, "My God, My God, why have You forsaken Me?" (Matt. 27:46). This was the key moment in Jesus' life—the moment for which He came. This was the moment He anticipated in Gethsemane when He prayed, "My Father! If it is possible, let this cup pass from Me. Yet not as I will, but as You will" (26:39). This was the moment when He drank the cup of His Father's wrath for all of us and became the substitutionary sacrifice for our sins.

What did Jesus' cry signify? For sure, it indicated the physical and emotional agony Jesus experienced on the cross. It also indicated His feeling of separation from God as He experienced the curse of sin. Interestingly enough, this is the only time in the New Testament where Jesus did not address God as "Father."

But through it all, this cry demonstrated Jesus' confidence in the midst of His agony. His cry was the first verse of Psalm 22, a psalm that begins with despair yet ends in victory (Ps. 22:24). Even while Jesus faced the wrath of God, He did so with confidence and peace, trusting God's righteous protection (1 Pet. 2:23).

That's why Jesus gave up His own life. It was not taken from Him. Matthew 27:50 says He "gave up His spirit." Emphasizing the same point, Luke records, "And Jesus called out with a loud voice, 'Father, into Your hands I entrust My spirit.'" (Luke 23:46). John underscores Jesus' authority over His own life as well when he recounts Jesus' last words—"It is finished!" (John 19:30).

The Gospels call us to believe in a suffering Messiah. But the Gospels do not present a Messiah overcome by His suffering. Yes, He was afflicted, accused, and hung on a tree at the hands of sinful people. But Jesus showed throughout His life that He was in control. When the time came, He left with the Roman guards, stood before Pilate without defense, and declared that He would *give* His life in love. It would not be taken from Him.

This is the Messiah we put our faith in for salvation. In the way He died, He revealed that He is the King, the Priest, and the Sacrifice. The sufficiency of our salvation depends on the suffering self-giving love of our Messiah. We have a great King, a faithful High Priest, and an unblemished Lamb in whom to put our faith.

Conclusion

In response to His death and resurrection, Jesus invites us to follow Him in His mission. He wants us to trust in His identity as the Messiah and in the work He accomplished on the cross.

It's in accepting that He is the Suffering Servant who gave His life for us that we find the courage to sacrifice for His mission. Only then do we have the assurance to lose our life for His sake, knowing that we can obtain true life in Him (Matt. 16:25). If we want our lives to be marked by following Jesus in His mission, we must put our faith in Jesus as the self-giving King who laid down His life for us.

PRAYER OF *Response*

Our Father, we dare call You by that blessed name, for we feel the spirit of children. We love You, we trust You, and we desire in all things to be obedient to Your will, and to seek Your honor.

All our dependence is placed on You since the day when You taught us to believe in Jesus Christ and now, You are all in all to us, You are our fullness, and we lose ourselves and find ourselves completely in You.

We would lie in the very dust before You because of sin; and yet, at the same time, rejoice in the great Sin-bearer, that the sin is not imputed to us, that it is put away by His precious blood, that we are accepted in the Beloved. But even this does not content us; we are crying after the work of the Holy Spirit within, till Satan shall be bruised under our feet, and sin shall be utterly destroyed.

This is our soul's grandest desire, that Jesus' name be lifted high, and His throne be set up among the people, to the praise of the glory of His grace. [3]
–Charles Spurgeon, adapted

Devotions

FOOLISH CROSS

The identity of the Messiah has long been a puzzle for many people—from the first-century religious leaders and Jesus' own disciples to those today who don't believe God became man and cannot fathom how He could willingly suffer and die.

Paul addressed the challenge of accepting Jesus as the Messiah in 1 Corinthians 1:18-25. He said Christ crucified was a stumbling block to the Jews. It was a stumbling block because it was an impossible idea. Israel long anticipated the coming of the Messiah to overthrow their enemies and establish His kingdom. The Old Testament prophecies spoke of His power and how He would establish the throne of David forever (Isa. 9:6-7). Never would they imagine that His victory would be won through a cross.

Paul also said the cross was foolishness to the Greeks because a dying King is a display of weakness, not strength. How could the Greeks worship a man who had been crucified on a cross?

But God's wisdom does not fit in our box. We want a powerful Messiah who serves our desires and overthrows the enemies that trouble us the most. Jesus has done so (Col. 2:15), but the Enemy He defeated is not always the enemy we are most concerned about. He has defeated Satan, sin, and death.

Being a disciple means boasting in the cross, no matter how bizarre it may seem to the world. It is what opens the door to the riches of God's wisdom.

Pause and Reflect

1   Are there times when you desire a different type of Messiah? Where are you tempted to look past Jesus' greatest work for you and dwell on other things you would really like Him to do for you?

- -

2   Take a moment to boast in the cross. Thank God for freely giving us His Son. Ask Him to keep you from being deceived by desires for a different king.

New Promises

On the night Jesus was betrayed and arrested, He made a startling claim to His disciples. He took the Passover meal and directed the disciples' attention to Himself, claiming to be the One to whom the Passover pointed.

The author of the Book of Hebrews explained that Jesus' blood established a new covenant (Heb. 9). The old covenant had to be fulfilled because it did not change the hearts of God's people. They continued to sin and rebel against God.

But Jesus offered Himself as the perfect sacrifice. He lived a perfect life, gave His life for us as a sacrifice, and now sits at the right hand of God as our great High Priest. When we accept His sacrifice and give our lives to Him, our sins (past, present, and future) are remembered no more. We are changed by the Spirit of life.

This simple gospel message should give us great joy and peace as well as a heart bursting with thanksgiving toward God. He did what the old covenant was unable to do (Rom. 8:2-3).

This simple gospel message should make us want to follow Jesus even more faithfully. When we realize what it means for us to receive the benefits of the new covenant, we rest assured in all of God's promises, and we desire to be obedient to Him. In short, through the message of the gospel, the Spirit forms us into the image of Jesus Christ.

Pause and Reflect

1   How is the simple truth of the gospel affecting you during this time of your life? Where do you see growth in your life because of your faith in the simple message of the gospel?

- -

2   Spend time thanking Christ for what He did for us. Confess any sins that come to mind, and express again your full trust in Jesus. Praise God for the promises in the new covenant.

The True Hero

John 13:35: "By this all people will know that you are My disciples, if you have love for one another."

When reenacting battle scenes in the backyard, boys rarely leap at the role of "sacrificial friend." When playing Cinderella in their rooms, little girls aspire to the beautiful, dancing princess and not the lowly servant girl constantly under the woes of her family.

Likewise, when it comes to living as a disciple of Christ, we usually choose to resemble the triumphant, judge, warrior-King Jesus and not the meek, lowly, humble, serving, sacrificial Christ. However, time and again, Scripture tells us to do good to "the least of these" (Matt. 25:40) and to serve one another (John 13:14).

Jesus tells us that it isn't our victories or our power that validate our union with Him but rather our love for others (John 13:34-35).

We tend to aspire to the role of hero, not servant. But when we have a true encounter with the Hero of creation's story, we are freed to make much of Him and not ourselves. We are free to show others love because we've been shown love in Christ. We are free to show others mercy because we've received great mercy from God.

Our love for others is the evidence that the love of God abides in us. Our service for others is fueled by the unimaginable way Jesus served us. His great love for us energizes our love for others (1 John 4:19).

Pause and Reflect

1   In your relationships to others, do you tend to take the posture of the "warrior-King" or the "humble servant"?

- -

2   Do you more often use others for your purposes or seek ways you might make much of them even at great sacrifice to yourself?

- -

3   Do you tend to promote your good deeds to others or do you tend to promote the welfare of others?

DISCUSSION QUESTIONS

1 Have you ever been in a situation in which people misunderstood the nature of your role and authority? How did you correct the misconception?

------

2 What kind of misconceptions and misunderstandings about Jesus' person and work are common in our day? How do the Gospels correct these misconceptions? Why is it important not only to understand how other people view Jesus but also to come to our own conclusion about His identity?

------

3 How do people in society today seek to make Jesus in their own image? How do churchgoers remake Jesus in our own image? How central is the cross to your understanding of who Jesus is? In what ways is taking up one's cross connected to following Jesus in His mission?

------

4 Describe a time when you had to pay the cost of following Jesus (socially, financially, a friendship)?

------

5 What might be some reasons for the Passover celebration being the time for Jesus' suffering and death? In what ways was the Passover event a picture pointing forward to Christ?

------

6 What are some differences between the old covenant and the new covenant? Why are the new covenant promises considered better? How might these better promises produce in us joy, peace, and assurance?

------

7 Jesus knew He would suffer the curse of sin. So why did He ask God why He had forsaken Him? What might be the reasons for such a piercing question?

------

8 The fact that God brought redemption out of the darkest of days means He is also working to bring good out of the suffering we go through (Rom. 8:28). How does the cross of Christ provide comfort during trials?

------

9 What do we learn about our salvation from Jesus' last words on the cross? How can these words strengthen our faith?

------

10 In what ways does Christ's sacrifice for us compel us to sacrifice our comfort in order to reach others with the good news of forgiveness?

Chapter 5

The Resurrection

The Resurrection and Exaltation of King Jesus

VOICES FROM *Church History*

"Christianity is in its very essence a resurrection religion. The concept of resurrection lies at its heart. If you remove it, Christianity is destroyed." [1]
–John Stott (1921-2011)

VOICES FROM *Church History*

"On the third day the friends of Christ coming at daybreak to the place found the grave empty and the stone rolled away. In varying ways they realized the new wonder; but even they hardly realized that the world had died in the night. What they *were looking* at was the first day of a new creation, with a new heaven and a new earth; and in a semblance of the gardener God walked again in the garden, in the cool not of the evening but the dawn." [2]
–G. K. Chesterton (1874-1936)

Many of the world's great stories include some sort of resurrection scene. From epic adventures like *The Lord of the Rings* (Gandalf the Grey to Gandalf the White) and *The Chronicles of Narnia* (Aslan) to classic fairytales like *Snow White* and *Sleeping Beauty*, the formula is the same: a battle that ends with the triumph of good over evil and life over death.

There's a reason these stories resonate with us. It's because they mirror the true story of the world. They testify indirectly to the resurrection of Jesus Christ as the pivotal moment of world history. But whereas many of these stories see resurrection as the happy ending, the Bible describes Jesus' resurrection as the new beginning. Because of Christ's resurrection, we are forgiven, set free from sin, empowered to worship God with our lives, and incorporated into Christ's resurrection people.

In this chapter, we will look at the reality of Christ's resurrection, the meaning of this event according to the Scriptures, and how it leads us to be on mission for God's kingdom. We'll also explore the truth of Jesus' ascension into heaven, where He sits at the right hand of the Father interceding for us as we await His return. As citizens of Christ's kingdom, we move forward with resurrection power to live according to His reign.

The risen King is victorious over death (Luke 24:1-8).

1 *On the first day of the week, very early in the morning, they came to the tomb, bringing the spices they had prepared.* 2 *They found the stone rolled away from the tomb.* 3 *They went in but did not find the body of the Lord Jesus.* 4 *While they were perplexed about this, suddenly two men stood by them in dazzling clothes.* 5 *So the women were terrified and bowed down to the ground.*

"Why are you looking for the living among the dead?" asked the men. 6 *"He is not here, but He has been resurrected! Remember how He spoke to you when He was still in Galilee,* 7 *saying, 'The Son of Man must be betrayed into the hands of sinful men, be crucified, and rise on the third day'?"* 8 *And they remembered His words.*

Imagine what must have been going through the minds of Mary Magdalene, Mary the mother of James, and the others after Jesus was crucified: *What next? Is there any hope? How could this have happened? This was so unjust! We thought He was the Messiah.*

On Sunday morning, the first day of the week, these ladies got up early to attend to Jesus' body. As they made their way to the tomb, they were stricken with grief. Their hopes for God's kingdom had been dashed. They had endured the trauma of losing their beloved Teacher.

Though their morning began with a sorrowful walk to honor their Teacher, everything suddenly changed—they did not find the body! Grief gave way to confusion. They saw two men in "dazzling clothes." Confusion gave way to terror. They heard, "Why are you looking for the living among the dead?" Terror gave way to joy. They realized the truth of Jesus' promise. Joy gave way to mission. The ladies ran off to tell the disciples.

The women rejoiced at the news. Something extraordinary had happened—death had died and Christ was alive! That's why the angels asked, "Why are you looking for the living among the dead?"

The angels helped the women understand through their astonishment by using the words of Jesus from before. Calling the women to remember, the angels said, in effect, "Don't take our word for it, take His! He said to you, 'The Son of Man must be handed over to sinful men, be crucified, and rise again on the third day.'"

How can we understand the meaning of the resurrection? Not just *that* it happened but *why* it happened and *what* this event means?

Biblically speaking, death follows disobedience. Take, for example, Genesis 3 and the sin of Adam and Eve. The next four chapters are marked by death. In Genesis 4, Cain killed Abel. Then Cain feared for his own life (4:14). "Then he died" is the refrain of the genealogy in Genesis 5. Then in Genesis 6–7, death and destruction touched the whole earth as God judged through the flood. Death is an inescapable reality even though God's creation was originally designed for life to flourish.

In the New Testament, Jesus Himself grieved the reality of death. He wept in the presence of Mary and Martha when His friend Lazarus died (John 11:32-35). His display of emotion expressed both compassion for His friends but also grief over death. He wept because death is an intrusion, a tool in the hands of the Evil One, something that holds all humanity in fear and slavery (Heb. 2:14-15).

So what does the resurrection of Jesus mean? Remember the connection between death and disobedience. If death is defeated, our disobedience has been dealt with. Earthly judges condemned Jesus, the innocent One, to the cross. But the Judge of heaven, God Himself, vindicated Jesus by raising Him from the dead. When we trust the verdict of God over the verdict of men, we too are vindicated along with Jesus. His life is our life. His obedience is counted as our own.

What were the effects of the resurrection in the lives of these women? They rejoiced. They remembered. They reported. We might expect them to hang around the tomb, to try and prolong the experience. But that's not what the women did. The resurrection was a call to action! News like this had to be told.

Imagine this scenario: Everything happens just as Luke tells it through verse 8—and then nothing else follows. About two weeks later, Peter and John see Mary Magdalene in the market. Peter asks, "Mary, what happened to you after the death of the Lord? Did you ever get to anoint the body?" "Didn't I tell you?" Mary replies. "Jesus rose from the dead that morning!" We can't even fathom the story moving forward in that way. The news of the resurrection is too explosive!

To really grasp the reality of the resurrection, we must be witnessing Christians. How could it be otherwise? We rejoice. We remember. We report!

The risen King is recognized by the disciples and validated by Scripture (Luke 24:36-49).

36 *And as they were saying these things, He Himself stood among them. He said to them, "Peace to you!"* 37 *But they were startled and terrified and thought they were seeing a ghost.* 38 *"Why are you troubled?" He asked them. "And why do doubts arise in your hearts?* 39 *Look at My hands and My feet, that it is I Myself! Touch Me and see, because a ghost does not have flesh and bones as you can see I have."* 40 *Having said this, He showed them His hands and feet.* 41 *But while they still were amazed and unbelieving because of their joy, He asked them, "Do you have anything here to eat?"* 42 *So they gave Him a piece of a broiled fish,* 43 *and He took it and ate in their presence.*

44 *Then He told them, "These are My words that I spoke to you while I was still with you—that everything written about Me in the Law of Moses, the Prophets, and the Psalms must be fulfilled."* 45 *Then He opened their minds to understand the Scriptures.* 46 *He also said to them, "This is what is written: The Messiah would suffer and rise from the dead the third day,* 47 *and repentance for forgiveness of sins would be proclaimed in His name to all the nations, beginning at Jerusalem.* 48 *You are witnesses of these things.* 49 *And look, I am sending you what My Father promised. As for you, stay in the city until you are empowered from on high."*

The disciples dispersed after Jesus' arrest and crucifixion, but news from the Marys began to get out. What's more, Jesus Himself appeared to His disciples. As they encountered Him, hope and joy were reborn in their hearts. In Luke 24:13-35, two disciples on their way to Emmaus began to process what had happened, trying to make sense of it all. As they walked, Jesus appeared to them, but they did not recognize Him.

Jesus inquired into their topic of conversation. They explained that they had been following someone they thought would redeem Israel but who had been crucified and buried. And now the body had gone missing. Jesus responded to all this by explaining that it was necessary for the Messiah to suffer (v. 26), suggesting that suffering did not disqualify Him from being the Christ. He made this point by showing how the Old Testament Scriptures actually pointed to a suffering Messiah (v. 27).

Though they did not completely understand, they were curious. So they urged him to stay and eat with them. During dinner, their eyes were opened, and they finally recognized Him. Once they did, He vanished from their sight. With hindsight, the two disciples asked each other, "Weren't our hearts ablaze within us while He was talking with us on the road and explaining the Scriptures to us?" (v. 32). In other words, *How did we miss that it was Him all that time?* Then they rushed to tell the good news to the other disciples in Jerusalem.

When these disciples joined the others, they discovered that Jesus had already appeared to Peter (vv. 33-34). They heard about the resurrection, and then they added their own testimony (v. 35). It became clear to them that the risen One was the One who had held up bread and wine just days before and said, "This is My body and blood for you."

Jesus then appeared to them all. In this moment, there seemed to be some anxiousness among them regarding the resurrection. Evidently, as they processed everything, new questions and doubts surfaced. So when Jesus came to them, His first words to this group were "Peace to you!" The disciples were "startled and terrified," Luke tells us. Jesus picked up on this and asked them, "Why are you troubled?"

We see in the disciples' actions that their confidence in a resurrected Jesus grew over time as Christ continued to appear to them. By the time we see the disciples in the Book of Acts, they are a resolved group, willing to die for their belief that Jesus is the Christ. But from these earliest days all the way to His ascension, some of them wrestled with doubt (Matt. 28:17).

It's encouraging to see that the "process of belief" for the disciples was very similar to the "process of belief" for many of us today. Even as we believe, we wrestle with moments of doubt. We are sometimes like the father who brought his son to Jesus in Mark 9. When Jesus said to him all things are possible for those who believe, he replied, "I do believe! Help my unbelief" (v. 24).

Jesus was gracious in His response to the disciples' doubt. He gave physical evidence for His physical resurrection. He encouraged them to touch Him and to see that He had flesh and bones (Luke 24:39-40). He pointed to His hands and His feet, which bore the marks of the nail prints. He was saying in this, "My body is real, like the body you knew before My death." Finally, Jesus ate some fish, showing yet again that His body was a real physical body (vv. 41-43).

The evidence compelled and convinced the disciples. Their disposition changed from startled and frightened, troubled and doubting, to joy and amazement.

For the third time in Luke 24, we are told that the Scriptures were fulfilled in Jesus' death, burial, and resurrection (vv. 6-7,26,46). Jesus affirmed three things the Scriptures teach about Him: the Messiah would suffer, the Messiah would rise, and repentance and forgiveness of sins should be proclaimed in His name to all nations (vv. 46-47).

Take a look at these three things. Notice which ones had already happened and what was still to come. Jesus had been crucified. He had been resurrected. But the forgiveness of sins and repentance still had to be proclaimed to the nations. With this list, Jesus took what had to happen to Him according to the Scriptures and connected it to what His disciples must do in order for the Scriptures to be fulfilled. Jesus was giving a mandate for missions. He said, "I've been teaching you that I must die and be raised. Now that that has happened, you are to go to all nations to proclaim the forgiveness of sins."

Notice that Jesus made another promise: "I am sending you what My Father promised" (v. 49). He promised to send the Holy Spirit. We are not left alone in the mission!

The risen King is enthroned and exalted over all creation (Luke 24:50-53).

At the beginning of this Gospel, Luke tells us about a number of godly people crying out to God in song and prayer for Him to send His salvation to His people. Remember Zechariah and Elizabeth, John the Baptizer's parents? Remember Simeon and Anna? Remember Mary's song? Luke records all those things and the song of the angels at the beginning of his Gospel as His people cry out for God to send salvation. Luke recorded 24 chapters about how God sent Jesus. He started with Mary's (the mother of Jesus), Zechariah's, and the angels' songs. He began the conclusion to his Gospel with the Marys hearing from the two angelic men that Jesus had risen from the dead. The hopes and joys of God's salvation are in full expression at the end of Luke's Gospel as Jesus ascends to heaven. So the new hope and joy that came with the news of the resurrection become settled and confident hope and joy as He leaves them and returns to His Father.

50 *Then He led them out as far as Bethany, and lifting up His hands He blessed them.* 51 *And while He was blessing them, He left them and was carried up into heaven.* 52 *After worshiping Him, they returned to Jerusalem with great joy.* 53 *And they were continually in the temple complex praising God.*

Jesus' ascension does not receive as much attention as other aspects of His life. We celebrate His birth because that is when God became man. We celebrate His sacrificial death because we receive forgiveness of sin. We celebrate His resurrection because death is defeated and our new life is won. But for most Christians and churches, that is where it stops. Very little thought is given to Christ's ascension to the right hand of God the Father.

For Luke, the ascension was a significant moment in the disciples' personal transformation and the advance of the gospel through the church. He emphasized the importance of the ascension by ending his Gospel with this event and beginning his second volume, Acts, with it.

The ascension had a profound impact on the disciples. Up to the moment that Jesus ascended to heaven, the disciples seemed to be puzzled, trying to figure it all out. But after the ascension, they worshiped Him. They traveled back to Jerusalem with great joy. They maintained a regular presence in the temple—worshiping God.

At first, the disciples' reaction to Jesus' ascension may catch us off guard. Jesus had just "left them." And yet they were happy—filled with joy. Why this reaction? After all, when Jesus told them at the end of John 13 that He would soon leave them, they were deeply disturbed. Thus, He encouraged them by teaching them about the ministry of the Holy Spirit (John 14–17). He kept them from the brink of utter despair by saying, "You are not losing Me, but I am going to be with you in a different way through My Spirit."

The ascension of Jesus produced joy because the disciples realized what amazing benefits would come to them when Jesus returned to the Father. When Jesus ascended, all the promises regarding the Spirit's ministry to the disciples were about to be fulfilled. The disciples accepted His ascension, for they had accepted Jesus' word about the promised One to come. Their doubts and fears were gone. They were convinced of who He was. They knew that He died to forgive them of their sins. They knew He was alive from the dead. In His resurrection, they had hope in victory over death. They trusted Him. For these reasons, Jesus' departure gave the disciples joy.

The benefits of the ascension are many:
- When Jesus ascended and sat down at the Father's right hand, the Father verified the accomplishment of the life, death, and resurrection of Jesus and confirmed that the final payment for sin had been made (Heb. 10:11-14).
- When Jesus ascended, the intercessory work of Jesus on behalf of His people began. In this ministry, we are assured that we will always have access to the Father forever (1 John 2:1).
- When Jesus ascended, His eternal reign over all enemies began. As Peter wrote, "Now that He has gone into heaven, He is at God's right hand with angels, authorities, and powers subject to Him" (1 Pet. 3:22).
- Finally, when Jesus ascended, the church was empowered to accomplish its mission. In Ephesians 1:22-23, writing about Jesus' resurrection and ascension, Paul said, "[God the Father] put everything under His feet and appointed Him as head over everything *for the church*, which is His body, the fullness of the One who fills all things in every way."

Jesus Christ is the King of the universe, and Satan can do nothing about it. What Satan *can* do is tempt us to forget about Jesus as King. He uses a thousand tricks to do it, but he is after one thing—to eclipse our present awareness of who Jesus is and where He is. In the Book of Acts, Stephen, right before being stoned, looked up into heaven and saw Jesus standing at the right hand of the Father. The New Testament points us to this picture so that we will have a settled confidence that Jesus our Savior is the King over all things.

Conclusion

Joy, hope, and mission are three consistent responses of the disciples to Christ's resurrection and ascension. In light of these two great events, we see the disciples transformed and mobilized to follow Jesus on His mission.

We go forward with hope and joy because the King of the universe promises that He will never leave or forsake us. If we want to experience greater transformation and the joy of following Jesus on mission, we should build our confidence on the finished and sufficient work of Jesus Christ. The resurrection and ascension testify to the completion and perfection of His work.

Devotions

MAKEOVER

Romans 8:23: "We ourselves who have the Spirit as the firstfruits—we also groan within ourselves, eagerly waiting for adoption, the redemption of our bodies."

Do you ever want to just scrap everything and start over? A new house—one that stays clean and everything is fixed. A new town—one where people don't know so much about you. A new job—one that excites you every day and is free of stress.

Whenever life gets challenging, you might just think, *I should sell everything and buy an RV. I should get out of Dodge and start over.* We might give this a thought or two, but we probably wouldn't do it. Too much to lose in starting all over again.

Ever wonder why God did not just start over. Does God have anything to lose? So why didn't He just start over when sin entered the world through the disobedience of Adam and Eve? It seems like that would be easier, does it not?

We learn something important by examining what God did instead. Sin placed God's good creation under a curse and in futility. Rather than throwing up His hands, God promised a coming Messiah who would restore all of creation. God destroyed sin, which was destroying us. He grants us life from death.

God does not start over because He has a greater plan. He plans to redeem and restore all things. He does not demonstrate His power by starting over. He demonstrates His power by reclaiming His creation for His purposes. So when you consider quitting, remember God does not quit. What He starts, He will complete (Phil. 1:6).

Pause and Reflect

1   Are you tempted to give up in an area in your life? Is it because you've failed too many times?

- -

2   How can God's plan to restore everything strengthen you to remain faithful?

Gospel Turning Points

Luke 24:32: "So they said to each other, 'Weren't our hearts ablaze within us while He was talking with us on the road and explaining the Scriptures to us?'"

Have you ever been struggling with despair and discouragement only to suddenly have your mind filled with gospel truth that lightens your heart?

Perhaps you've been fighting temptation when suddenly the truth of Christ's cleansing blood for you took away the enticement toward that sin. Or maybe you have been self-focused and self-absorbed only to have God graciously lead someone into your life who needs serving and caring for.

Moments like these are gospel turning points. They change our outlook on life. The Spirit uses these moments to remind us that we are in the presence of the victorious King of the universe. Even more, because of the gospel, His victories are ours! These are powerful spiritual encounters where God opens spiritual eyes to see the glory of Jesus.

Hundreds of things in our lives can distract us from seeing Jesus as our victorious King. We get blinded to His glory. Cares, fears, desires, ambitions, hurts, and stress points can all turn our heads and keep us from seeing Him. But as Paul explains in 2 Corinthians 4:6, God can awaken us. He shines light into our hearts to open our eyes to the supremacy of Christ. When we encounter the risen Christ, we are assured of His love and commissioned for His kingdom.

Pause and Reflect

1   Consider what in your life might be distracting you from knowing the presence of God in your life.

- -

2   If God's presence is known when we put our hope in the gospel, what can you do today to help you trust Jesus and believe the gospel promises?

GREAT MISSION, GREAT POWER

Think about the power and might of God. He is Creator, Sustainer, and Savior. Think about how God has demonstrated His power. He spoke the universe into existence. He sent a flood that destroyed the earth. He rained sulfur and fire down on Sodom and Gomorrah. He "plagued" Egypt 10 times and delivered Israel by damming up the Red Sea. He demonstrates great power, unmatched power.

Then consider the cross and the resurrection. In these events, the spiritual forces opposing God were overthrown—defeated (Col. 2:15). In redemption, God shows tremendous power and might. He defeats death with death. He gives new life to His people through the life of His Son.

Now pause and hear the words of Paul in Ephesians 1:18-20: "I pray that... you may know...the immeasurable greatness of His power to us who believe, according to the working of His vast strength. He demonstrated this power in the Messiah by raising Him from the dead and seating Him at His right hand in the heavens."

Paul is praying that we might know that God's amazing power is working *in us* and *for us*. The fact that God's power is given to us in the Holy Spirit and that God would choose to use it through us is incredible. He compares this power to the very power that He demonstrated in the resurrection of Christ.

Why does God work His great power in us and for us? It is because God has called us to join Him in mission. The church, as the body of Christ, is called to proclaim the reign of Christ over all things (Eph. 1:22-23).

Pause and Reflect

1   Do you regularly experience God's power working in you and for you?

- -

2   What is one reason you may not be experiencing God's power in you?

DISCUSSION QUESTIONS

1   What are some resurrection themes you see in books and movies? What about in nature? How do they compare and contrast with the truth of Christ's resurrection?

2   In what ways does Christ's resurrection represent a *new beginning* rather than a *happy ending*? Why is this distinction important?

3   How did the truth of the resurrection change the way the followers of Christ viewed His life and work? What does the resurrection mean for our own understanding of Jesus and His mission?

4   What role do the emotions of awe, wonder, and joy play in our sharing the good news of Christ's death and resurrection?

5   What hope does the truth of Christ's resurrection give us when we are facing death? What other areas of life are influenced by the events of Easter morning?

6   Why do we experience moments of doubt even as we believe? What difference does it make to our faith that Jesus comes with such graciousness in our doubting?

7   How does Christ's patience with the disciples encourage us as we help others in various stages of their spiritual walk?

8   Jesus connected His death and resurrection and the church's mission to the fulfillment of Scripture. How does the truth that our mission is grounded in all of Scripture mobilize and motivate us in our work for the kingdom?

9   Why do you think the church does not give much attention to the ascension? Why was the ascension a turning point for the disciples in relation to their mission? In what ways can the ascension similarly affect the church today?

10 How are the different spheres of life (family, work, recreation, government) affected by the truth of Christ's reign over all?

Part 2

GOD'S NEW COVENANT PEOPLE

After Jesus' ascension, the Holy Spirit came to indwell believers, to constitute a new community of faith, and to empower the spread of the gospel. In the power of the Spirit, Peter and the disciples boldly proclaimed the gospel and people responded in repentance and faith and were baptized. Through the Spirit-empowered work of the church, the gospel spread from Jerusalem to the ends of the earth, uniting believers from every tribe, tongue, and nation into one, grace-shaped family of faith, which displays to the world the power of the gospel.

Chapter 6

Pentecost

God Indwells His Covenant People

Recently I decided to try my hand at doing minor repair work on our family vehicle. The only problem? I waited until evening to begin the project, which meant I would be attempting the task in the dark, aided only by a flashlight I rounded up from inside the house. The flashlight was the perfect size and weight for the project. But there was one snag—dead batteries. I had a flashlight with everything necessary for proper operation (including LED bulbs that seem to last forever) but no way to power the light without a source of energy.

Even in our best moments, when we think we are prepared and ready for the task of following Jesus, the prospect of failure seems very real. Just think of Jesus' disciples. Unlike us, they had walked physically with Him, had learned from Him, and had encountered Him in His glorified and resurrected body. But even *they* needed supernatural power to fulfill His mission. Knowledge and experience alone did not prepare the disciples to carry the mantle of their Teacher.

All of this brings me back to that flashlight. It was perfectly suited for the task at hand, yet it failed to produce light for the same reason that the disciples were unable to fulfill Christ's mission on their own—no power to achieve the goal.

Previously we celebrated the news of Jesus Christ's resurrection from the dead and His ascension into heaven. Just before His ascension, Jesus instructed His disciples to wait in Jerusalem "for the Father's promise" (Acts 1:4)—the Holy Spirit, who would empower Christ's disciples to be His witnesses on earth.

In this chapter, we will see how the promised Holy Spirit descended upon Christ's disciples. As we witness the work of the Holy Spirit in the early church, we will see how the Spirit indwells those who believe in Christ, empowers believers to spread the gospel, and builds up believers into the community of faith.

The Holy Spirit indwells every believer (Acts 2:1-4).

In the early days of human history, there was only one language spoken on the earth. As the world began to be repopulated following the great flood, some of those who moved eastward devised a plan to build a city with a tower reaching into the sky. They wanted to create a monument to glorify themselves and to keep from being "scattered over the face of the whole earth" (Gen. 11:4). This was in direct disobedience to God's command to "fill the earth" (9:1). As a result, God confused their language, which forced them to stop building the tower. Their city was known as Babel, or Babylon.

Fast-forward a few thousand years, and we discover another scene in the Bible with confusion caused by the speaking of various languages. This time, it's Jesus' followers. But instead of confusion leading to the scattering of people, this event leads to the gathering of people.

1 *When the day of Pentecost had arrived, they were all together in one place.* 2 *Suddenly a sound like that of a violent rushing wind came from heaven, and it filled the whole house where they were staying.* 3 *And tongues, like flames of fire that were divided, appeared to them and rested on each one of them.* 4 *Then they were all filled with the Holy Spirit and began to speak in different languages, as the Spirit gave them ability for speech.*

In many ways, the Holy Spirit's work on the Day of Pentecost constituted the reversal of Babel. Whereas in the Old Testament the confusion of languages led to the scattering of the people of the world, in the New Testament the coming of the Holy Spirit paved the way for a new community—a people who transcend the barriers of nationality and unite around the cross and resurrection of Jesus Christ.

This is not the first passage in Scripture that attests to people being filled with the Holy Spirit. However, this giving of the Spirit is unique, just as John the Baptizer prophesied in Luke 3:15-16 about Jesus: "He will baptize you with the Holy Spirit and fire." John the Baptizer represented the last of the prophets of the old covenant era, and he pointed to Jesus as the One who would usher in a new era of God's work.

In the old covenant era (the Old Testament), the Holy Spirit came upon men and women in order to empower them for the work God had called them to accomplish, but His work was not on such a grand scale. (That's why at one point Moses expressed his desire for every person in Israel to be prophets, that "the LORD would place His Spirit on them!" [Num. 11:29].) Something else we see in the Old Testament is the possibility of the Holy Spirit's power being removed from those who rejected the covenant standards of the nation of Israel (see 1 Sam. 16:14; Ps. 51:11).

So when God promised to establish a *new* covenant, He also promised to give His Spirit. And the nature of the Holy Spirit's work would be different in the new covenant than in the old. How? *All* who belong to God because of the work of Jesus Christ receive the Holy Spirit's indwelling presence. And furthermore, the Spirit's presence is not only life-giving and mission-empowering but also *permanent*.

The Federal Deposit Insurance Corporation (FDIC) was created in 1933 by the federal government as a guarantee to insure against loss up to $2,500 dollars of a bank account's deposits—a number that has increased over time, up to $250,000 in 2010. The guarantee of this promise is the "full faith and credit of the U.S. government." If the government fails to live up to its obligation, then its own faith and credit would be in jeopardy.

In a more powerful way, the Holy Spirit guarantees the reality of God's promise to redeem everyone who believes the gospel. That's why the apostle Paul would later write that believers are "sealed with the promised Holy Spirit...the down payment [deposit] of our inheritance, for the redemption of the possession, to the praise of His glory" (Eph. 1:13-14).

If the promise of salvation is not fulfilled, then the full faith and credit of God Himself is at stake. Because salvation is the gracious promise of God received through faith, God takes upon Himself the sole responsibility of carrying out His Word.

The indwelling presence of the Holy Spirit is one of the most beautiful gifts of Christ's saving work. Every believer receives this gift, just as they receive forgiveness of their sins. The indwelling of the Holy Spirit is evidence that you are truly a believer (Rom. 8:9). Because God dwells in us, the Holy Spirit acts as the deposit, the guarantee of final salvation.

The Holy Spirit empowers the spread of the gospel (Acts 2:22-36).

22 *"Men of Israel, listen to these words: This Jesus the Nazarene was a man pointed out to you by God with miracles, wonders, and signs that God did among you through Him, just as you yourselves know.* 23 *Though He was delivered up according to God's determined plan and foreknowledge, you used lawless people to nail Him to a cross and kill Him.* 24 *God raised Him up, ending the pains of death, because it was not possible for Him to be held by it.* 25 *For David says of Him:*

I saw the Lord ever before me;
because He is at my right hand,
I will not be shaken.
26 *Therefore my heart was glad,*
and my tongue rejoiced.
Moreover, my flesh will rest in hope,
27 *because You will not leave me in Hades*
or allow Your Holy One to see decay.
28 *You have revealed the paths of life to me;*
You will fill me with gladness in Your presence.

29 *"Brothers, I can confidently speak to you about the patriarch David: He is both dead and buried, and his tomb is with us to this day.* 30 *Since he was a prophet, he knew that God had sworn an oath to him to seat one of his descendants on his throne.* 31 *Seeing this in advance, he spoke concerning the resurrection of the Messiah:*

He was not left in Hades,
and His flesh did not experience decay.
32 *"God has resurrected this Jesus. We are all witnesses of this.* 33 *Therefore, since He has been exalted to the right hand of God and has received from the Father the promised Holy Spirit, He has poured out what you both see and hear.* 34 *For it was not David who ascended into the heavens, but he himself says:*
The Lord declared to my Lord,
'Sit at My right hand
35 *until I make Your enemies Your footstool.'*
36 *"Therefore let all the house of Israel know with certainty that God has made this Jesus, whom you crucified, both Lord and Messiah!"*

How could a man who had denied Jesus three times out of fear for his life stand before a crowd of thousands and proclaim the gospel in such a powerful and forceful way? It seems incredible, and indeed it is. But it's exactly what we see on the Day of Pentecost when Peter stood before the crowd and preached the gospel. How was this possible?

The answer points us to the reality and purpose of the Holy Spirit's presence. Now that we've seen the truth that the Holy Spirit indwells believers, it's time to explore the reason *why*. And it's in discovering the reason for the Holy Spirit's work that we begin to grasp the vital element in understanding how the Holy Spirit works in our lives today.

Guiding Believers

When Jesus taught His disciples about the Holy Spirit, He explained how the Holy Spirit would work in their lives. One aspect of the Holy Spirit's work was that He would "guide you into all the truth" (John 16:13).

The full effect of this ministry of the Spirit would become evident when the church struggled with the gospel's expansion into the Gentile world. The Spirit's leadership directed the church to accept all who believed the gospel, thus ensuring the good news would truly be taken to the ends of the earth. He continues this important work today as He leads God's people through His Word, which is why we can trust the Scriptures as the truth of God upon which to build our lives.

Reminding Believers

Another vital role that the Spirit would have was to "teach you all things and remind you of everything I have told you" (John 14:26). Have you ever tried to remember the details of a conversation that took place a few years ago? The further you are removed from an event, the less you will remember the specifics.

How can we be sure that the teachings of Jesus happened as they did when so much time has passed from the time they were first heard? The power of the Holy Spirit ensured that the disciples would be supernaturally reminded of everything they needed in order to pass along the words and works of Jesus. And we trust that the Spirit will bring to our minds the Word of God we have treasured in our hearts.

Empowering Believers for Mission

Most clearly in this passage, we see how the Holy Spirit enabled Peter to preach the gospel powerfully and persuasively, leading to a sense of conviction among the men and women in the crowd. Peter's boldness was a clear result of the work of the Spirit in his life. The fear he had exuded on the night of Jesus' arrest had been replaced with the power of God.

Peter's message was delivered through the power of the Spirit; the conviction of the people took place through the power of the Spirit; and the salvation of all who believed was only possible through the power of the Spirit. Likewise, it is our responsibility to share the gospel, but it is the Holy Spirit who empowers us to do so.

That's why, as a Christian, you have nothing to fear! Everything needed to fulfill the commission of Christ to preach the gospel is available to you through the power of God's Spirit. The pressure is off, for salvation is the work of God alone. We are His mouthpieces, commissioned to share the message of eternal life and empowered and emboldened by the presence of the Holy Spirit in our lives.

The Holy Spirit builds the community of faith (Acts 2:37-42).

37 *When they heard this, they came under deep conviction and said to Peter and the rest of the apostles: "Brothers, what must we do?"*

38 *"Repent," Peter said to them, "and be baptized, each of you, in the name of Jesus Christ for the forgiveness of your sins, and you will receive the gift of the Holy Spirit. 39 For the promise is for you and for your children, and for all who are far off, as many as the Lord our God will call." 40 And with many other words he testified and strongly urged them, saying, "Be saved from this corrupt generation!"*

41 *So those who accepted his message were baptized, and that day about 3,000 people were added to them. 42 And they devoted themselves to the apostles' teaching, to the fellowship, to the breaking of bread, and to the prayers.*

"What must we do?" The answer to this question determines everything. How could the men and women who were declared guilty of the death of God's Son and Messiah possibly do anything to repair the breach in relationship? Peter's message was bold. And through his preaching of the gospel, the Holy Spirit convicted those who were listening.

The same is true for us today. The gospel message calls for a two-fold response. The first response is *repentance*—a turning from sin and an exchange of allegiance as we confess Jesus as Lord. Our allegiance to Christ should not be seen as a work added to His work. Instead, it is the new direction we go in once we have turned from sin and surrendered to the authority of King Jesus. When we repent, we receive forgiveness of sins and the gift of the Holy Spirit.

If you were traveling down the road and became aware that the direction you were headed was leading you to certain death while another route led to certain life, then you would need to decide which path you would follow. Simply being aware of another route is not enough to prevent the outcome of your current direction. In the same way, when the gospel is preached, we are confronted with our current path of sin (which leads to destruction) and the path of Jesus (which leads to eternal life). Repentance is a direction-change grounded in the revelation of the gospel.

The other response demanded by the gospel is *faith*. If repentance displays a proper attitude toward sin, then faith is the trust of one's life and eternity to Jesus for the forgiveness of sins. This forgiveness provides salvation from the effects of sin, including our rebellious alienation from God, physical and spiritual death, and the coming wrath of God. Faith and repentance are our response to the Spirit's conviction as He makes unbelievers aware of their need for salvation through the preaching of the gospel (Acts 5:31; 11:18).

Without the gospel, we are hopelessly lost. But God has looked upon us with love and has given us the hope of new life in spite of our evil condition. And when we repent and believe, we enter into a restored relationship with God that is the work of the Holy Spirit.

Peter also connected repentance and faith to the expression of baptism. Believers show their faith by being baptized. It should not be assumed that baptism somehow merits salvation. The Scriptures make it clear that salvation is by grace (unearned favor in spite of our sin) through faith (our repentant belief that God alone can save). But baptism is very important as it is the sign we belong to God's people. Do you see what the Holy Spirit was doing at the Day of Pentecost? He was empowering Christ's followers as they proclaimed the gospel.

He was breaking down worldly barriers to that message so that all present could hear and understand the good news. He was convicting people of their sin and leading them to repent and believe. And through it all, He was building the church as people were baptized.

What exactly is the church? Most people think the word refers to a physical structure or an institution. However, the Greek word *ekklesia*, the word from which we translate *church*, refers to an assembly of "the 'called-out ones' of God."[3] Broadly speaking, the church of Jesus Christ is the community of those who have entered into relationship with God through the work of Christ. Therefore, the foundation of the church is the gospel, and it is through the power of the Spirit that the church is built.

Acts 2:41-42 lays out the characteristics that mark the local church. A local church is made up of people who believe the gospel and have been baptized. It is also marked by a commitment to the teaching of Christ through His apostles. (In the Great Commission, Jesus commanded His disciples to teach believers to obey everything He had commanded" [Matt. 28:20].) The church is also devoted to fellowship and breaking bread with one another—signs of their devotion to one another as members of the new covenant community. Lastly, a church must be devoted to prayer, which demonstrates our reliance upon God to lead the church according to His will.

Conclusion

It's easy to get distracted when reading the miraculous account of Pentecost. Some people focus all their attention on the speaking in tongues but miss how Peter connected this miracle to the fulfillment of God's promise of salvation for everyone who called upon the name of the Lord. The main point of this account is the Spirit-empowered proclamation of the gospel message.

Supernatural signs such as tongues, miracles, and even resurrection, if they are separated from God's message, are not enough to convince people of God's salvation. The miracle of tongues may have intrigued the crowd, but it was the powerful message of the gospel that ensured the crowd's salvation.

Conversion itself is a miracle. But the Spirit's power doesn't stop there. We move forward with the promise of the Spirit to fill us and empower us. Just as God has provided everything we need for salvation, so He has provided everything we need to accomplish His mission.

Devotions

WHEN YOU DON'T KNOW
WHAT TO SAY

Have you ever found yourself in a situation where you didn't know what to say? Maybe you heard some shocking news, or maybe you saw something so profound that you couldn't put it into words. Perhaps you were speechless at the precise moment you were supposed to deliver a message.

Sometimes we don't share the gospel because we worry we might mess it up or we might not have all the answers. There are times I have found myself speechless out of fear. Sometimes it's because they may reject what I have to say. Other times I am afraid that I will say the wrong thing in an effort to make the Bible more palatable to those who don't know Christ.

Jesus promised His disciples that the Holy Spirit would give them the words to say when He presented opportunities for proclaiming the good news. If we truly believe that the Holy Spirit is empowering us, including the words we speak on His behalf, then we have something more powerful than fear. We also know that we do not have to speak on our own, for He is with us.

When we surrender to the Spirit of God in our lives, we do not have to fear evangelism. We should be fearful when we approach it without relying on God's Spirit, as is the case whenever we try to take the edge off of the truth. Still, we learn from these moments that God is faithful, and He will give us new opportunities to rely upon Him to tell others the greatest story ever told!

Pause and Reflect

1   Examine your heart and consider any reasons that make you hesitate when sharing the gospel.

- -

2   In John 14:25-27, why did Jesus say that we don't have to be afraid? Why is it important to remember that the Spirit not only gives us confidence but also the right words?

When You Don't Know What to Pray

The most basic definition of prayer is communicating with God. However, it can be stressful when you focus on saying the right thing. After all, you are praying to the Creator of the universe!

That's why we can be grateful for the indwelling presence of God's Spirit, who intercedes on our behalf. When we pray, God's Spirit communicates our desires to God. But He has an advantage that we do not have. Because He is God, He knows what His will and plan is. So even when our prayers may not line up with God's will, God's Spirit helps us by taking our desire to do God's will and praying for God's will to be done on our behalf.

One of the principles of the Lord's Prayer is "Your will be done" (Matt. 6:9-13). When we pray with this attitude, we are expressing that we are seeking God's will above our own wants and desires. The Holy Spirit's power extends to our own weakness in prayer, and He bridges our communication gap by expressing our heart to God (Rom. 8:26-27). When we submit to the Holy Spirit, our prayers will change us as we begin to express our childlike thoughts to our Father.

As the perfect Father, He does not give us everything we want, but He does answer our prayers in accordance with His will, which is always for our good and His glory. Prayer reminds me that I am not powerful or knowledgeable to accomplish anything, and it humbles me that I need the help of God's Spirit in my life as I pray.

Pause and Reflect

1 What is your greatest struggle when it comes to prayer?

---

2 How would believing that God knows your desires better than you do help you become less fearful about praying for the wrong thing?

Unity in Diversity

When I was a sophomore in college, I was given the opportunity to travel to India and Thailand as part of a mission team. I was humbled by the poverty of so many in the city of Calcutta. One particular woman is etched in my memory. As we were being transported by bus, I watched out my window as a mother was walking in the crowded street holding her infant child. I looked ahead and saw another bus coming the opposite direction with very little room to pass beside us, much less beside a mom carrying her baby. Without stopping, the two buses passed one another with so little space between them that I could have reached out and tapped the mother on her head.

As we continued to drive through the city, there were many times that we were halted by large bulls that were resting in the streets. The honor shown to these animals was in stark contrast to the dismissive way that this mom and child had been treated on the very same streets. I couldn't understand how anyone could be treated so poorly, as though they had been dehumanized, while an animal could stop the flow of traffic in an instant.

Unfortunately, this is how some people in God's family are treated. They are looked at or treated as though they are less important based upon their race, gender, social status, or age.

Through the Spirit, there is a unity that is able to transcend our differences and bring about a community that reflects the diversity of the kingdom of God. (Read Gal. 3:26-29; Eph. 4:1-6.) No matter our background, physical characteristics, or talents, we are all in need of God's grace. When the world sees a church that is unified by the Spirit, they will see the love Jesus said would characterize His disciples.

Pause and Reflect

1   How have you seen barriers (age, gender, socio-economic, etc.) affect the church?

---

2   Why is it so important for believers to be unified in the Spirit?

Discussion Questions

1 Have you ever been discouraged at how difficult it seems at times to follow Christ? How do you respond to these times of difficulty? Recount a time in your life when you tried to do something in your own strength, without relying on the power of the Holy Spirit. What did you learn from that experience?

2 In what ways does your church reflect the heart of God who promises to build up His people? Why is it important for churches to transcend worldly boundaries in sharing and celebrating the gospel?

3 Why is it important that Christians work hard at making the gospel message accessible and understandable to unbelievers? How can we contextualize the message in a way that does not compromise its truth?

4 In what ways does the reality of the Spirit's life-giving, permanent presence in your heart affect your view of Christian living? How does the Spirit's work in your life provide you with assurance of salvation? Can you recall a situation when the Spirit reminded you of a passage of Scripture at an important moment of decision or during a conversation with someone else?

5 Is our lack of confidence in sharing the gospel indicative of a lack of faith in the Spirit's power? Why is it important to recognize the supernatural element of conversion?

6 Can you articulate the gospel as clearly as Peter does in Acts 2? How would you describe the concepts of *repentance* and *faith* to someone with no biblical knowledge or church background?

7 Why is it important to keep an individual response of repentance and faith connected tightly to baptism and church membership? What are the dangers of church-less Christianity?

8 How clearly are the marks of the church in Acts 2:41-42 visible in your own congregation? What steps can you take as a group to make these marks more visible in your church?

9 Why is it important that churches pray? What does our corporate prayer life say about our reliance on the Holy Spirit's power?

Chapter 7

Our Identity

The Grace-Shaped Family of God

VOICES FROM *Church History*

"'What are these false apostles doing?' Paul cries. 'They are turning Law into grace, and grace into Law. They are changing Moses into Christ, and Christ into Moses. By teaching that besides Christ and His righteousness the performance of the Law is necessary unto salvation, they put the Law in the place of Christ, they attribute to the Law the power to save, a power that belongs to Christ only.'" [1]
–Martin Luther (1483-1546)

VOICES FROM *Church History*

"Holiness is not the way to Christ. Christ is the way to holiness." [2]
–Adrian Rogers (1931-2005)

"Amazing grace! how sweet the sound That saved a wretch like me!" These well-known words were penned by John Newton, a former slave trader turned pastor, who never recovered from the amazing grace he received from God. Newton's life is a testament to the nature of grace. Nothing about his past made him a worthy candidate for salvation, and yet a former slave trader (himself a slave to sin!) was set free by the grace of God.

Grace is a hard concept for us to understand because it does not operate according to our notions of fairness. Our attitude toward others could best be summed up as "If you do what I want, then I will grant you my favor." That's why, whenever we do certain prescribed actions, we expect to receive what we have earned.

And so we go about thinking life should be fair, all the while recoiling at the thought of receiving everything we *actually* deserve when we mess up. We say we want everything to be equal, but deep down we really want to be treated as the exception, not the rule. We yearn for fairness at the same time we yearn for grace.

Simply defined, grace is unmerited favor. In the Scriptures, it refers to the act of God giving His Son on behalf of a rebellious world in order to adopt undeserving people into His family through faith, which enables them to become heirs of His kingdom. Grace is scandalous because it seems unfair and because it unites people from diverse backgrounds around the gospel of Jesus Christ.

In this chapter we look at how the early church dealt with a controversy over what constitutes a true believer in Christ. At stake in this discussion was the nature of grace. In Jerusalem, the apostles came together to proclaim that the church is united by faith in Christ's work on the cross and by the fruit that flows from faith-filled hearts. Even today, sheer grace incorporates us into the family of God, shapes us as a people, and strengthens us for Christ's mission.

Works-based religion threatens the centrality of faith in Jesus Christ (Acts 15:1-5).

Previously we saw how the Holy Spirit moved in an extraordinary way at Pentecost. We saw how the message of the gospel resounded with people who spoke different languages and came from multiple places. In the following chapters in Acts, we see the gospel of Jesus going forth and bearing fruit among all kinds of people, not just the Jews. Once a persecutor of Christians, Paul became a missionary. He and Barnabas were commissioned by the church leaders in Antioch (Acts 13:1-3). They regularly preached in the synagogues, but they also saw many Gentiles who became followers of Christ.

At this point in the church's history, the majority of believers were Jews who had accepted Jesus as their promised Messiah. The question of whether Gentile believers were to be accepted into the faith community had already been settled (see 10:1–11:18). The answer was yes! But it was still unclear exactly how the early church should reconcile the observation of the ancient Jewish law with these new Gentile converts. What badges were necessary for new converts to prove their identity as part of God's people?

Every family has squabbles. They usually come down to insignificant differences that are easy to overcome. However, there are some crises that can threaten the very foundations of a family's survival. Divorce. Abandonment. Deception. Strong sibling rivalry. These occasions pose serious threats to the unity and health of a family.

Acts 15:1-5 records a major crisis that needed to be resolved in order to protect the church's unity and foundation for the new covenant family of God.

1 *Some men came down from Judea and began to teach the brothers: "Unless you are circumcised according to the custom prescribed by Moses, you cannot be saved!"* 2 *But after Paul and Barnabas had engaged them in serious argument and debate, the church arranged for Paul and Barnabas and some others of them to go up to the apostles and elders in Jerusalem concerning this controversy.* 3 *When they had been sent on their way by the church, they passed through both Phoenicia and Samaria, explaining in detail the conversion of the Gentiles, and they created great joy among all the brothers.*

4 *When they arrived at Jerusalem, they were welcomed by the church, the apostles, and the elders, and they reported all that God had done with them.* 5 *But some of the believers from the party of the Pharisees stood up and said, "It is necessary to circumcise them and to command them to keep the law of Moses!"*

What was this family squabble all about? Put simply, it was about who is in the family and on what basis. Imagine being part of a family where you are related by blood and share common characteristics and family traditions. Suddenly, your parents adopt some children who don't share the same ancestry. You wonder about these new "brothers and sisters" who don't share your traditions. What would it take for you to accept them?

The situation in Acts is similar. The Antioch believers associated with the Pharisees looked at these new "brothers and sisters" and said, in effect, "You'll be one of us as soon as you undergo the rites and uphold the traditions of our family."

Circumcision was a rite that God initiated as a sign of His covenant with Abraham (Gen. 17), and it was codified in the commands given by God to Moses (Lev. 12:2-3). For Jewish believers in Jesus, their identity was still heavily connected to their Jewish heritage. Circumcision was a matter of national pride, and it connected Jewish men to the heritage of their forefathers.

Paul and Barnabas, however, saw the situation differently. In their view, the Gentile believers didn't need to be circumcised in order to be part of the family. *They already were part of the family because of their faith in Jesus.* Salvation had been accomplished on the basis of God's work, not their own.

What appears on the surface to be a little tiff about what it means to be part of God's family reveals at its root a fundamental misunderstanding of the gospel. Instead of viewing salvation as being a gift of sheer grace and received by faith, some were saying that salvation came through grace plus obedience to the law of Moses. In other words, they believed the basis of salvation was Christ *plus* something else (in this case, circumcision).

The issue at stake was the very message of the gospel. If circumcision was to be made a requirement for Gentiles to enter into God's family through Christ, then the demands of the whole Jewish law would have been required for salvation (Acts 15:7-11). Christianity would have become a tribal religion that nullified the work of the Spirit at Pentecost.

To respond to this crisis, a delegation including Paul and Barnabas was sent from Antioch to the apostles and elders in Jerusalem. This gathering is often referred to as the Jerusalem Council, or the first church council. The early church leaders declared that in light of Christ's work, circumcision was not required for salvation. Neither was it required to be "part of the family." Instead, faith in Jesus alone is what constitutes God's people.

We cannot miss the importance of this debate. If our religious efforts are necessary to achieve salvation, then the perfect life of Jesus, His death for our sins, and His resurrection are not the sole provision for our rescue. If our salvation is earned (even partially) through our own righteousness, then grace is nullified since grace is unmerited favor and cannot be earned. Not only that, it would mean the church is united around something other than faith in Christ.

Once we base our salvation on our own righteousness, we remove God from the center of the story and put ourselves in control of our eternal destiny. Even more, we start boasting in our own accomplishments. The gospel ceases to be good news because it makes us out to be good people who simply need help, not helpless people who need rescue.

Works-based religion is contrary to saving faith because it diminishes the accomplishment of Christ. Our salvation comes through believing that Jesus was our perfect substitute upon the cross and that His victorious resurrection defeats the stranglehold of sin and death. To add anything to Christ's work is to turn salvation into something that we have earned in return for our good behavior instead of the gracious gift of a loving God.

The Jerusalem Council declared boldly that salvation is not on the basis of works. The leaders stepped into the family squabble and said, "You are brothers and sisters in Christ—not because you are Jews, not because you are circumcised, and not because you have a history together but because of your faith in Jesus. Don't put up unnecessary boundaries when you call people to repent and to trust in Christ's work alone."

God's people are constituted by grace alone through faith in Jesus alone (Gal. 2:15-21).

The church in Galatia dealt with the same issue facing the Jerusalem Council. Certain leaders were saying that Gentiles needed to observe the works of the law in order to be saved and considered a true member of God's people. In fact, even the apostle Peter withdrew from certain Gentile believers at the table, implying that the basis for fellowship was ethnic identity and not Christ. In his letter to the church, the apostle Paul—a Jewish man himself—boldly declared the meaning of Christ's work.

15 *We who are Jews by birth and not "Gentile sinners"* 16 *know that no one is justified by the works of the law but by faith in Jesus Christ. And we have believed in Christ Jesus so that we might be justified by faith in Christ and not by the works of the law, because by the works of the law no human being will be justified.* 17 *But if we ourselves are also found to be "sinners" while seeking to be justified by Christ, is Christ then a promoter of sin? Absolutely not!* 18 *If I rebuild the system I tore down, I show myself to be a lawbreaker.* 19 *For through the law I have died to the law, so that I might live for God. I have been crucified with Christ* 20 *and I no longer live, but Christ lives in me. The life I now live in the body, I live by faith in the Son of God, who loved me and gave Himself for me.* 21 *I do not set aside the grace of God, for if righteousness comes through the law, then Christ died for nothing.*

Herein lies the problem of relying upon "works of the law" to provide salvation: The law was never intended to bring salvation! God gave the law for several reasons, including to show our own inability to fulfill His righteous standard. Jesus confronted the Pharisees as being whitewashed tombs because they appeared law-abiding on the outside but were dead on the inside. The law can address our behavior, but only the gospel can address the sinful condition of our hearts. If a right standing before God can come through obedience to the law, then Jesus' death was in vain.

Paul emphasized that we are justified before God as a result of grace received through faith. None of us can enter into the family of God apart from God's initiating work of grace and our faith-response to the gospel. Instead, we must be "crucified with Christ"—dead to the law and alive toward God, just as Paul wrote.

Earlier we looked at the human desire to be treated fairly *and* with grace. How is that possible when it comes to salvation? How is it fair for God to give us what we deserve *and* show us grace? The answer is in the cross and resurrection of Jesus Christ. By giving Christ what we deserve, we are given grace. God upholds His justice and shows His love at the same time.

When we are justified ("declared righteous"), Christ takes our sin and we receive His righteousness. When God looks upon those who have believed in the gospel, He sees us as holy because of the perfect sacrifice of His Son in our place. This is why Paul could say that he continued to "live by faith in the Son of God." Our lives are changed by this grace. We never "get over" the gospel as followers of Jesus. Knowing Christ not only saves us but also sustains us. Paul held up the giving of Jesus, motivated by love, as the greatest evidence of the grace of God.

In dying with Christ, Paul was saying that his life was no longer defined by keeping the law. He was now defined by the life of the Savior. Faith is the doorway by which we know and experience the grace of God. Saving faith lets go of any vestiges of works-based righteousness that may remain in us, and it identifies us solely with what Christ has done on our behalf to make us righteous sons and daughters by grace through faith.

God's people are marked by faith in Jesus alone that results in good works (Jas. 2:18-26).

Both Paul and James (the brother of Jesus) were present at the Jerusalem Council in Acts 15. We've seen how Paul affirmed the truth of justification by faith alone in his letter to the Galatians. Now we see a letter from James and a passage that, at first glance, seems to contradict Paul.

18 *But someone will say, "You have faith, and I have works." Show me your faith without works, and I will show you faith from my works.* 19 *You believe that God is one; you do well. The demons also believe—and they shudder.*

20 *Foolish man! Are you willing to learn that faith without works is useless?* 21 *Wasn't Abraham our father justified by works when he offered Isaac his son on the altar?* 22 *You see that faith was active together with his works, and by works, faith was perfected.* 23 *So the Scripture was fulfilled that says, Abraham believed God, and it was credited to him for righteousness, and he was called God's friend.* 24 *You see that a man is justified by works and not by faith alone.* 25 *And in the same way, wasn't Rahab the prostitute also justified by works when she received the messengers and sent them out by a different route?* 26 *For just as the body without the spirit is dead, so also faith without works is dead.*

It looks like James is contradicting everything we have discussed to this point. How can the teaching of James be reconciled with the Jerusalem Council? Were the teachings of Paul and James in opposition to one another? This issue is of great importance because Paul declared a curse upon anyone, including himself, who preached any other gospel than the one he preached (Gal. 1:6-9).

The more we look at this passage, the more we see that Paul and James are like two swordsmen standing back to back battling off opposing enemies. Paul is battling the group that says works must be added to faith for salvation. James is battling the group that says faith for salvation doesn't lead to works.

Imagine this scenario: I come to you announcing that I've spotted a tornado and that the only way to stay safe is to follow me to an underground shelter. If you told me that you believed me and wanted to live but then decided to stay where you were, I would rightly question the nature of your trust in me to keep you safe.

Saving faith will always affect our behavior, and this is the point that James was making in these verses. When James said that Abraham was justified by works, he was not contradicting the Scriptures that say Abraham was counted righteous through his belief in God (Gen. 15:6). So just what *was* James saying?

Simply put, James was contrasting faith as mental assent to truth and faith as absolute trust in God's salvation. Demons know and believe in God, and it causes them to tremble, but they are not moved to action as a result of their faith. Saving faith is more than simply subscribing to truths about God. Faith that places absolute trust in Christ for salvation will result in good works. These are not the works of the law that Paul said are incapable of saving anyone, but they are works that come as the result of faith.

For James, being justified carried the connotation of evidence of something that has already taken place. This is why he pointed to Abraham offering Isaac as justifying him by works. It was not a saving act, but it was evidence of the righteous declaration of God that was made earlier because of Abraham's faith.

Abraham's obedience proved that his faith was not merely assenting to truth about God. His actions proved his trust in God's promise to make him into a great nation. Abraham's faith was so certain, he even believed God could raise Isaac from the dead, which was evidenced by his willingness to give up the son of promise (Heb. 11:17-19).

Works are not the cause of salvation, but they are the fruit of salvation. They do not precede our justification by faith alone through grace alone, but they certainly result from the decisive act of God in our lives.

Conclusion

Some family spats are worth having, particularly when there are major issues at stake. The Jerusalem Council reaffirmed the truth that salvation by grace alone through faith alone distinguishes followers of Jesus from all other religious groups. Only the gospel of grace has dealt with the underlying problem of human sin in a way that upheld God's perfect standard of holiness, provided forgiveness, and established relationship with God apart from the law.

For those of us who have received grace, it is essential that we treat others with grace. Grace does not provide a license for sin; rather, it provides the most excellent motivation for obeying Jesus—undeserved love being lavished upon those who at one time were His enemies.

- -

HYMN OF *Response*

"Marvelous, infinite, matchless grace,
Freely bestowed on all who believe;
All who are longing to see His face,
Will you this moment His grace receive?
Grace, grace, God's grace,
Grace that will pardon and cleanse within;
Grace, grace, God's grace,
Grace that is greater than all our sin."
–Julia H. Johnston

Devotions

THE NATURE OF FAITH

Read James 2:14-26; Ephesians 2:8-10.

Did you know Satan and his demons are believers? While their existence is spent trying to thwart the plan and purposes of God, they believe all that the Scriptures say. They are not misinformed or ignorant of their actions. Nor are they unaware of their ultimate destiny. Their belief is simply knowledge of the truth, and even this causes them great fear. They are characterized by conscious rebellion against the Creator of the universe.

It is this kind of "faith" that James so adamantly opposed. He confronted a kind of believing that accepts something as true without being changed by the truth. What would you think of me if my wife and children wore dingy clothes, were starving, and lived in a cardboard box while I lived in a mansion, had a personal chef, and wore custom-tailored suits? I could tell you that I love my family, but my actions would be evidence of a different reality.

According to Paul, we are not merely saved from sin but we are saved to do good works that glorify God. This is the signature of a life marked by the saving work of Christ. Just as the characteristic brush strokes on a painting can identify the artist, so the characteristics of saving faith identify the workmanship of God in our lives. We are saved by faith alone in Jesus, but our faith does not stand alone. Faith that saves leads to truth in action, and it inevitably results in the good works we were created *in Christ Jesus* to accomplish. The gospel ensures a new way of life for those who believe the truth.

Pause and Reflect

1   What is the relationship between faith and works?

- -

2   What role do good works play in the life of a Christian?

Shocking Grace

Read Luke 15:11-32; Romans 5:6-8.

The story of the prodigal son gives me great hope. This younger son abandoned his family, essentially wished his father dead by asking for his inheritance, and lived a life of such wickedness that it would be hard to find its equivalent. If anyone deserved to be cast away, forgotten, and treated with contempt, it was this son.

However, the son came to his senses when he found himself craving the scraps being fed to pigs. Few things would have been as revolting to a Jewish individual as sharing the trough of an unclean animal. If ever there was a lost cause, this son was it. As Jesus told the story, you can imagine that His audience never would have expected the twist Jesus threw at them.

The father not only took his son back but he had spent the days watching and waiting for his son to return. Grace broke through the pain and humiliation the father had endured, and he brought his boy back with celebration. Such is the shocking nature of grace.

We are the wayward, wicked son. God is the offended father. And the grace shown is a picture of the grace we receive in salvation. When we are brought into the family of God, it is easy to forget what we have been rescued from, including our own self-righteousness (see the older brother).

We must never forget that grace is so amazing because it is so shocking. Grace and love were shown "while we were *still sinners*," and it gives hope because there is no one too far gone to receive the lifeline.

Pause and Reflect

1   With whom can you identify in the story of the prodigal son? Why?

- -

2   How does Romans 5:8 underscore the shocking nature of grace?

THE MATH DOESN'T ADD UP

Read Matthew 20:1-16.

Put yourself in the shoes of the day laborers. Can you imagine getting paid the same amount for a full day of labor as those who only worked an hour? Personally, I would be incredulous at such treatment, and it seems as though the employer in this parable was not aware of workplace equity. The story illustrates grace in a powerful way, and it points out that the issue we struggle with most when it comes to grace is the tension between fairness and generosity.

Our attitude toward others could best be summed up as "If you do what I want, then I will give you my favor." We want what we have earned, but we recoil at the thought of receiving what we actually deserve when we fail to live up to the standard set before us. If we are honest with ourselves, we want to be treated better than we deserve. Thankfully, the math of grace is not based upon the rules of fairness, or we would all be in trouble.

In Christ, God has shifted the balance in our favor. Without grace, nothing would be to our advantage. Our family, religious pursuits, and especially our good works have no power to succeed in dealing with the underlying problem of our sinfulness versus God's standard of absolute perfection. Grace is important because it is the only remedy God could grant that would take us out of the equation altogether.

On the cross, Jesus received the fullness of God's wrath against our sin, which we deserved, and in His resurrection, we share in His victory over death, hell, the grave, sin, and Satan. Be glad that the math of grace doesn't add up, and joyfully side with the generosity of the gospel over against getting what we deserve.

Pause and Reflect

1   Why does grace seem unfair?

2   Do you struggle more with showing grace or being fair? Why?

Discussion Questions

1 Why is it we desire to be treated fairly *and* graciously at the same time? What does this tell us about our hearts and how we view ourselves?

2 Why is the idea of *Christ plus something else* dangerous? In what ways does adding to salvation distort our understanding of God and detract from Christ's glory? How would you describe the concept of *grace* to a non-Christian? What illustrations would you use?

3 What unnecessary boundaries do churches put up regarding repentance? What might unbelievers stumble over in our churches *before* getting to the offense of the cross?

4 How does the Jerusalem council's emphasis on faith alone for salvation impact our mission to take the gospel to all kinds of people?

5 How does knowing the purpose of the law change the way we read and study it? How does being declared righteous by grace alone through faith alone exclude works of the law from salvation?

6 If God has shown us grace through Jesus, how should this affect our interactions with other people in our lives? In what ways do you struggle with showing and receiving grace?

7 In light of the truth that God's people are established through faith alone, how ethnically diverse should our churches be? What does ethnic diversity (or the lack thereof) communicate about our view of the gospel?

8 What distinguishes saving faith from mere intellectual assent to facts about Jesus? Why is it so important that saving faith produces good works?

9 Is it possible to have assurance of salvation without bearing any fruit of the Spirit?

10 How does justification by faith alone free us to love our neighbor without seeking a reward?

Chapter 8

Our Mission

The Mission, the Message, and the Messenger

VOICES FROM *the Church*

"The Sender (God) delivered His message to us and then writes His message in us and through us for us to deliver to others. He sends us. We are His letter of love into the culture around us to the people whom He loved enough to die for. He asks us now to love in the same way." [1]
–Jason Dukes

VOICES FROM *Church History*

"Every friend of Jesus is a friend of missions. Where there is a healthy spiritual life, there is a love for the missionary cause." [2]
–Andrew Murray (1828-1917)

Most of us hear the word *missionary* and think of people who have left everything behind in order to tell others about Jesus. You may imagine dangerous encounters with tribal chiefs or smuggling Bibles into closed countries. Some of us may remember a person who came to our church and talked about their ministry in a foreign land. Unfortunately, few (if any of us!) hear the word *missionary* and picture ourselves.

When I was five years old, a missionary couple stayed in our home. They came to our church to share their story. This family had experienced the work of God firsthand in their missionary travels. Even if they never sought adulation for their ministry, I can remember looking up to them as "super Christians" because of their commitment to give up their lives for the gospel of Christ.

Of course, there is nothing wrong with holding godly men and women in high esteem or following their example. Paul suggested that Christians *should* look up to him as an example of godliness, as long as his life was reflecting Jesus. But there *is* a problem with creating a category of believers so committed to the gospel message that they will do anything (such as becoming a missionary) while expecting less from the rest of us believers. The truth is all of us are missionaries. God is a sending God, and His mission ought to be the directing passion of our lives.

The Book of Acts chronicles the spread of the gospel from Jerusalem to the ends of the earth. God's people are called to be on mission and are entrusted with the gospel message that is true for everyone, Jew and Gentile alike. The mission of the church is to make disciples by the power of the Holy Spirit. Moving from God through the church to the world, God's redemptive work results in people from every tribe, tongue, and nation responding in lifelong worship.

God's people are called to be on His mission (Acts 1:4-8).

4 *While He was together with them, He commanded them not to leave Jerusalem, but to wait for the Father's promise. "This," He said, "is what you heard from Me;* 5 *for John baptized with water, but you will be baptized with the Holy Spirit not many days from now."*

6 *So when they had come together, they asked Him, "Lord, are You restoring the kingdom to Israel at this time?"*

7 *He said to them, "It is not for you to know times or periods that the Father has set by His own authority.* 8 *But you will receive power when the Holy Spirit has come on you, and you will be My witnesses in Jerusalem, in all Judea and Samaria, and to the ends of the earth."*

The disciples experienced 40 days with Jesus after He was raised from the dead. Can you imagine their anticipation about what was coming next? As witnesses to the miracle of His resurrection, they no longer doubted Jesus was the Messiah. They were also confessing Him as their Lord and God (John 20:28)—the King to conquer the final enemy of death (1 Cor. 15:26).

Having encountered Jesus' power, they asked a question they must have wondered about throughout Jesus' ministry: Is the nation of Israel going to be restored to its glorious place as the chosen people of God? This question was rooted in the Old Testament concept of the Day of the Lord. When the Day of the Lord would come, Israel's adversaries would be overthrown, and God's kingdom would be established through His people. The disciples were reflecting the prevalent belief that the promised Messiah would be the One to establish this kingdom.

Unfortunately, their focus, just like ours tends to be, was smaller than the mission God was calling them to. For the disciples, the nation of Israel had become the focus of the story, just as we so often try to make ourselves the focus of the story. The disciples were asking Jesus if Israel would be restored to prominence, but Christ's response focused on the trajectory of God's mission moving forward.

To understand Jesus' answer concerning God's mission, we must return to Genesis. It was in the garden of Eden that God initiated His rescue mission of redemption following the disobedience of Adam and Eve. He revealed His worldwide intentions when He called a man named Abram and promised to make him into a great nation (Gen. 12:1-3). However, God did not stop with a single nation, for His promise was to bless many nations through Abraham's descendants.

Jesus wasn't saying anything new; rather, He was bringing attention back to the scope of God's mission from eternity past. He was telling His disciples, "*You* (children of Israel) are not the point of what you are experiencing." God's plan had always been to bless the world through the descendants of Abraham. Israel had a unique calling to be God's missionaries to the world, but they traded this mission for conformity to their pagan neighbors.

In the Great Commission, Jesus gave His disciples clear directives for being His witnesses to the ends of the earth. They were to make disciples, baptize new believers, and teach them to obey Jesus' commands (Matt. 28:19-20). Again, the emphasis was upon *all* nations. Jesus was sending His disciples out as missionaries to the world, not just to their fellow Israelites.

Missionaries are those who are sent by God to carry out His mission. We follow the model of Jesus, who Himself was sent by the Father to the world (John 20:21).

The Book of Acts focuses on the actions taken by the apostles in response to the commission they received from Jesus. The second half of Acts focuses on Paul's travels throughout the Roman Empire to take the gospel where it had not been heard and to plant churches. He was set apart by God as the apostle tasked with missionary work to the Gentiles, and his story is an amazing testimony of a life solely committed to God's mission.

Through the missionary journeys of Paul and others, the gospel began to take root throughout the Roman Empire, and the good news spread toward the ends of the earth. You and I are beneficiaries of these believers' obedience, and we honor them and our Lord by continuing their obedience in taking the gospel to the world.

God's people are entrusted with His message (1 Cor. 1:18-25).

Before his conversion, Paul was known by his Hebrew name, Saul. He was a Pharisee who was zealously pursuing the one true God revealed in the Scriptures. When a new sect came on the scene claiming that a man named Jesus was the Messiah, Saul began to persecute them violently. The first mention he receives in Scripture is at the stoning of Stephen, where he is shown giving his approval to the actions of the crowd (Acts 7:54–8:1). He then proceeded to inflict torment upon the church of God and was well known by the Christians as an enemy of the gospel.

Prior to his salvation, Saul was aware of the crucifixion of Jesus, but he saw the cross as a foolish way for God to provide forgiveness of sins. As a member of the Pharisees, he believed in a final resurrection but rejected the resurrection of Jesus, for this would have vindicated His identity as the Messiah.

But something changed for Saul as he was traveling to Damascus to continue his angry pursuit of Christians—He met the risen Jesus. This encounter would mark him forever. As he opened his letter to the Corinthian church, we can see Paul's old view of the cross compared to his new understanding.

18 *For the message of the cross is foolishness to those who are perishing, but it is God's power to us who are being saved.* 19 *For it is written:*
I will destroy the wisdom of the wise,
and I will set aside the understanding of the experts.

20 *Where is the philosopher? Where is the scholar? Where is the debater of this age? Hasn't God made the world's wisdom foolish?* 21 *For since, in God's wisdom, the world did not know God through wisdom, God was pleased to save those who believe through the foolishness of the message preached.* 22 *For the Jews ask for signs and the Greeks seek wisdom,* 23 *but we preach Christ crucified, a stumbling block to the Jews and foolishness to the Gentiles.* 24 *Yet to those who are called, both Jews and Greeks, Christ is God's power and God's wisdom,* 25 *because God's foolishness is wiser than human wisdom, and God's weakness is stronger than human strength.*

As Paul traveled throughout the Roman provinces preaching the gospel, he encountered many cultures that prized wisdom and knowledge. Compared to their debates on the meaning of life, Paul must have sounded rather foolish. I'm sure he experienced his fair share of blank stares, ridicule, and mistreatment.

If you've ever been in a situation where you wanted your message to be accepted, then you've probably felt the pressure of trying to tailor what you have to say for the people you want to impress. Paul must have been tempted to change the message of the gospel to be more palatable for his hearers, to minimize the risk of alienating them with its content. Thankfully, though, Paul never seemed to be too concerned with public opinion. God's opinion mattered more.

In Acts 18, we see Paul's first journey to preach in the city of Corinth, where he stayed for a year-and-a-half teaching and establishing the church. His message emphasized the death of Jesus on the cross, a bloody and vicious method of punishment reserved for the worst offenders of Roman law. Just as some today want to de-emphasize the nature of the suffering that Jesus endured upon the cross, it's likely that Paul was asked to "tone it down" because such discussions were unsuitable for polite company.

But Paul could not escape the truth that his former life of zealous persecution could only be pardoned by what he at one time considered foolish. The cross debases human achievement. All that Paul thought he was accomplishing for God was revealed as powerless to save. This is why the message of the cross is not only "foolish" but also "offensive" to people.

For the Jews, it was offensive to hear that they were involved in the murder of their long-awaited Messiah. It also offended them to be told they had misunderstood the Messiah's mission. For the Greeks, the message of "Christ crucified" offended their sensibilities. They thought it a barbaric, unenlightened way of describing deity. Whatever the reason, the cross always turns upside down our assumptions about God and His salvation.

At the same time, though Paul made it clear that the cross unites Jew and Gentile by offending them, the power of the cross also unites Jew and Gentile by saving them. Christ's work brings together people from various life experiences, nationalities, genders, and socio-economic backgrounds. Jews and Greeks may be equally offended, but it's also true that both Jews and Greeks can be saved! All who bow the knee to the crucified Savior are united by the power of the cross and resurrection to save us from sin.

The message is entrusted to us *as is*, and it should not be adjusted according to the sensibilities of modern culture. It is *God's* message and not our own. Paul could unashamedly proclaim the gospel because "it is God's power for salvation to everyone who believes" (Rom. 1:16). We too must be bold in proclaiming the simplicity of the message of the cross. When we do, God will take *His* offensive message and bring about salvation, thus proving His wisdom to those who believe.

God's people are called to be His messengers (2 Cor. 5:14-21).

As believers, we are called to obey Jesus' command to go into the world and preach the gospel. But what is the motivation behind our obedience? The apostle Paul dealt with our motivation by taking us back to the reality of Christ's love.

14 *For Christ's love compels us, since we have reached this conclusion: If One died for all, then all died.* 15 *And He died for all so that those who live should no longer live for themselves, but for the One who died for them and was raised.*

16 *From now on, then, we do not know anyone in a purely human way. Even if we have known Christ in a purely human way, yet now we no longer know Him in this way.* 17 *Therefore, if anyone is in Christ, he is a new creation; old things have passed away, and look, new things have come.* 18 *Everything is from God, who reconciled us to Himself through Christ and gave us the ministry of reconciliation:* 19 *That is, in Christ, God was reconciling the world to Himself, not counting their trespasses against them, and He has committed the message of reconciliation to us.* 20 *Therefore, we are ambassadors for Christ, certain that God is appealing through us. We plead on Christ's behalf, "Be reconciled to God."* 21 *He made the One who did not know sin to be sin for us, so that we might become the righteousness of God in Him.*

The driving force behind God's messengers is Christ's love for the world He came to save. John 3:16 is clear that God's love was the motivation for giving Jesus. That love now fills our hearts and becomes our motivation for giving of ourselves.

The selfless love displayed by Jesus in His life and death is Paul's reference point for our love for others. The love of God compels us to live for Him and to pour ourselves out for others. This was Jesus' desire (John 12:50), and it now becomes our own. We live for a resurrected God and Savior, not for ourselves, and this should press us into action.

Paul focuses our attention upon the spiritual dilemma that is solved only through the gospel. We do not see others "in a purely human way" because we recognize the necessity of new life that comes at conversion. The new creation that we become in Christ begins in the spiritual realm, not the physical realm. We will experience new creation bodies at the resurrection, but the work of the Holy Spirit begins by making our spirits, which were dead in sin, alive to God. We must begin seeing the lost around us as people who need new life.

Paul also makes clear that there is no Plan B for taking the gospel to the ends of the earth. God has chosen us for the task to be His ambassadors.

Almost every country has ambassadors—men and women who serve as representatives of their country's government. They give up lives in their homeland in order to live and work in the country to which they have been sent. Their responsibility is to communicate the messages given to them on behalf of their government.

When two countries are experiencing tension, it is not unheard of for an ambassador and his staff to be attacked. Why does this happen? Because ambassadors are a tangible representation of the message and policy of their nation. How they interact with the people of their host country can reflect either positively or negatively upon their nation. That's why they must take care to represent their fellow citizens well.

This is the picture Paul uses to explain our relationship toward those who need new life. We are ambassadors to the world with a message of reconciliation. God has made a way for sinful people to become His friends instead of His enemies. God has provided a pathway to peace in spite of the world's rebellion. The fact that God offers peace in spite of us, not because of us, is what makes this such good news!

So what do we do? We plead with others to be saved, in the same way that God would plead with them, which is what He is doing through us.

All of this—reconciliation, ambassadorship, life, and new creation—comes because of what Jesus did in our place. Because Jesus took upon Himself our sin, shame, and punishment, we receive God's righteousness, friendship, and mission. And now we serve as ambassadors for King Jesus!

Conclusion

Because God is a missionary God, He sends His people out on mission in order to spread the message of redemption that comes through His Son. The good news is we are not alone in this task. In Acts 1:8, Jesus promised the power of the Holy Spirit to carry out the mission, and in Matthew 28:20, He promised His presence. God does not need us for this mission, but He wants us to experience the overwhelming joy that comes through partnering with Him.

To experience the joy of God's mission, we must relinquish any sense of self-importance. Selfishness will constrict God's love in us. When we live in the love that we have received in Christ, we cannot help but overflow with love for the world. And so we spread the gospel with our lips and demonstrate the truth of the gospel with our lives.

Hear the missionary mandate of Jesus! Be ready to go across the street and across the world. We will accomplish the mission of God when the love of Christ so fully engulfs our hearts that sharing the gospel and loving others as Christ loved us become the natural expressions of our relationship with God.

PRAYER OF *Response*

"Savior of sinners, mobilize believers everywhere to share the Good News with the lost. Let our very lives be a testimony to Your love. Give us a passion for the lost, Lord, and a deep desire to share Your glorious Good News with those who haven't heard. As Jesus told us, Lord, we pray that You will send workers into the harvest. Give us a passion. Lord, send us! Like Isaiah, help us to say, 'Here I am. Send me.' Amen." [3]

Devotions

A GOD WHO CARES FOR SINNERS

Read Jonah 3–4.

Many of us are familiar with the story of Jonah being swallowed by a great fish. But how many of us have overlooked the background to this story? Jonah was told to go to the capital city of Israel's greatest enemy, the Assyrians. He was told to preach a message of impending destruction. Instead, Jonah ran in the opposite direction.

Surprisingly, the prospect of Israel's enemy being destroyed didn't sadden Jonah. He ran because he knew that if the people of Nineveh repented, then God would turn away His anger and forgive them for their evil deeds. He ran because he *didn't* want God to show His compassion toward the people of Nineveh. Jonah knew that God shows grace, mercy, and love to even the worst offenders of His law. Jonah displayed a selfish attitude toward people whom God loved. He wanted to keep God's grace for people like himself.

The story of Nineveh ended with a glorious picture of salvation, but Jonah's story ended with frustration. He was angry with God for being gracious to His enemies. He would rather have died than see the people of Nineveh escape the wrath of God. He cared more about a plant God graciously provided for him than for the souls of 120,000 people who were on the precipice of divine disaster.

The story of Jonah gives us a glimpse into the compassionate heart of God. Our God cares about people, and He lavishly pours out His grace upon any sinner who turns from sin and believes the good news of Jesus.

Pause and Reflect

1 In what ways do we exhibit Jonah's attitude toward the unsaved?

- -

2 What reason did God give for sparing the people of Nineveh?

THE INTERNATIONAL
FAMILY OF GOD

Read Revelation 5:8-14.

My wife and I love to walk around IKEA to get ideas for decorating various rooms in our house. One of the most interesting parts of the IKEA store near our home is its international flair. It is not uncommon to hear six or seven different languages being spoken in a single trip. Our trips there serve as a much needed reminder that the world is made up of a variety of nationalities, languages, and cultures. A humbling thought to say the least! It also reminds me of God's mission to redeem people from every part of the world.

I know individuals who show great disdain for people different from them. They don't like the language being spoken or the color of their skin or the different nationality. It is sad to hear anyone talk like this, but it is especially heartbreaking when those who feel this way claim to follow Jesus.

We must realize that Jesus offered Himself as a sacrifice for the sins of all kinds of people, regardless of race, color, creed, or language. The mission of God includes a host of people who don't look or sound like us and who don't share our common culture. God's mission is international in scope. If you are a believer in Jesus, then your family includes everyone who calls upon the name of the Lord. We are unified in our diversity through our shared belief in Jesus, the Savior of the whole world.

Pause and Reflect

1   Why do we struggle with people who are different from us?

----

2   How does the gospel unify us in spite of our differences?

MAGNIFICENT OBSESSION

Read Acts 9:1-20; Philippians 3:8-11.

Have you ever obsessed over something? Athletes obsess over their bodies and skills, and parents obsess over their children. Another word that comes to mind when I think of obsession is *zeal*. Zeal is defined as "passion for a person, cause, or object." Even if you have trouble thinking of yourself as being obsessed, at least you would have to admit that you have shown zeal for someone or something in your life.

Paul was familiar with obsession and zeal. He was so obsessed to do what he thought God wanted that he persecuted Christians. He wanted to rid the world of anyone who claimed that Jesus was the Messiah. He despised these people who claimed that Jesus had been crucified and had come back to life three days later. What transformed his zeal from destroying the church to telling others about Jesus?

The short answer: he encountered Jesus and found a new passion for his life. The problem with Paul wasn't that he lacked fervor. His problem was that in his zeal to make God pleased, he actually was fighting against God. Paul's zeal was replaced with the pursuit of a God who had passionately pursued him. Jesus changed Paul's perspective and his life. Jesus became Paul's obsession, which was the foundation for his obedient participation in the mission of God.

Like Paul, we must begin to love as God loves and do what God has done. He sent His Son, and now He has sent us to be missionaries to a world obsessing for all the wrong reasons.

Pause and Reflect

1 Who or what dominates your thoughts, feelings, and actions?

- -

2 What would happen if fulfilling God's mission became the zeal of your life?

Discussion Questions

1   What is the story of your conversion to Christ?

---

2   What jumps to your mind when you hear the word *missionary*? What keeps you from thinking of yourself as a missionary? How would thinking of yourself as a missionary change your view of the workplace? Your sports activities? Your finances?

---

3   In what ways are we tempted to trade our mission for a life of conformity to the world around us? What happens when we focus only on the benefits of our salvation and not our calling from King Jesus?

---

4   When you think of the mission of God, do you think in terms of God's global work or His local work? Why? How can we be involved in each sphere (global and local) of God's mission activity?

---

5   Why is it important to see God as a "missionary God"? How does this aspect of God's character affect our understanding of our mission?

---

6   What seems "foolish" or "offensive" about the gospel of Christ crucified and raised? What are some ways we may be tempted to downplay the foolish or offensive nature of the gospel in order to make it fit with modern sensibilities?

---

7   How can our churches uphold and prioritize the gospel message as being of first importance? How does your presentation of the gospel compare to Paul's in 1 Corinthians 1:18-25?

---

8   What happens when we are compelled by something other than love in our involvement in God's mission?

---

9   In what ways does your life reflect the priorities of ambassadorship for the kingdom of God? What would change if we saw ourselves (first and foremost) as those sent by God on His mission?

---

10   What resources does your church have that can be used for God's global mission? In what ways does your church enable you to be used for God's global mission?

Chapter 9

Our Unity

United in Truth, Clothed in Grace

VOICES FROM *Church History*

"The church is to be a loving church in a dying culture. How, then, is the dying culture going to consider us?...Upon His authority He gives the world the right to judge whether you and I are born-again Christians on the basis of our observable love toward all Christians." [1]
–Francis Schaeffer (1912-1984)

VOICES FROM *the Church*

"Your spiritual family is even more important than your physical family because it will last forever. Our families on earth are wonderful gifts from God, but they are temporary and fragile, often broken by divorce, distance, growing old, and inevitably, death. On the other hand, our spiritual family—our relationship to other believers—will continue throughout eternity. It is a much stronger union, a more permanent bond, than blood relationships." [2]
–Rick Warren

It's often said that churches split over insignificant issues: the color of the carpet, the style of music, or the proper dress code for worship services. I know of a particular church that split because some members wanted to relocate while others wanted to stay. Those who opposed the relocation put signs in their yards that said, "Keep our church alive!" We might be tempted to laugh off some of these examples were it not for the great harm these disputes do to our Christian witness.

Christians often approach church unity in one of two ways. The first approach focuses on believing the right information about God. The church is joined together in shared doctrine. This approach is characterized by unity grounded in truth. Unfortunately, there are times when unity in essential doctrines can be turned into uniformity in personal preferences. Truth gets emphasized to the neglect of grace.

The second approach focuses on having good relationships. The church is joined together because of the relationships they share with God and each other. Unfortunately, there are times when this view of grace gets distorted and no one is ever confronted for straying from the truth of God. It seems like, on the surface, everyone is nice and loving, but the biblical view of love is missing because truth has not been integrated into the church's relationships.

In this chapter, we will look at the necessity of both truth and grace as the foundation for unity among God's people. Each of the Scripture passages was written by the apostle Paul during his imprisonment in Rome. In these texts, we see that God's truth is the foundation of unity, that a strong focus on our mission as God's people helps us maintain unity, and that the gospel provides the example and the power for unity.

The foundation of unity (Eph. 4:1-6)

If you were imprisoned for your involvement in a righteous cause, what would you write to your family and friends? More than likely, since you'd have nothing to lose, you'd strip away everything else and zero in on the main issues you were passionate about. That no-nonsense approach tends to mark the many examples of letters and books that have been written from behind bars. From Martin Luther King Jr.'s "Letter from a Birmingham Jail" to Dietrich Bonhoeffer's *Letters and Papers from Prison*, these and other prison letters focus attention on the prisoner's cause.

The apostle Paul's prison literature was no different. Jailed for proclaiming the gospel with boldness, Paul wrote four short letters, each focusing on the glory of God's grace and how that grace changes the way we live.

While in prison, Paul wanted to remind his readers that they must walk worthy of the Lord who had called them to salvation. And it's clear he saw the church's unity as an important part of what it means to "walk worthy." Take a look at Ephesians 4:1-6.

> 1 *Therefore I, the prisoner for the Lord, urge you to walk worthy of the calling you have received,* 2 *with all humility and gentleness, with patience, accepting one another in love,* 3 *diligently keeping the unity of the Spirit with the peace that binds us.* 4 *There is one body and one Spirit—just as you were called to one hope at your calling—* 5 *one Lord, one faith, one baptism,* 6 *one God and Father of all, who is above all and through all and in all.*

Keep in mind that Paul was in prison when he wrote these words. He was suffering persecution for his obedience to Jesus. That's why he called himself a "prisoner for the Lord." This made his appeal to walk worthy of the calling even more critical for the Ephesian believers he was addressing. He called the believers to essential truths, for which he was in chains, and away from the petty divisions that so easily arise.

Do you see the way Paul jumped back and forth from speaking of gentleness, grace, and acceptance to unity in the core truths that bind us together? It appears he wanted us to be doctrinally sound and patient with one another. These were not mutually exclusive, as is clear in the example of Jesus Himself.

Jesus overturned the tables in the temple even as He extended grace to those trapped in sin. He refused to condemn the woman caught in adultery, but He also told her to go and sin no more. He interacted respectfully with the woman at the well, but He also told her to drink the living water only He could offer. He spoke truth to His disciples, changed tax collectors like Zacchaeus, and welcomed sinners and outcasts to His table. There is something wrong if we who follow Jesus are never characterized as firmly against sin yet humble and gentle with those who are sinners.

Paul's admonition to accept one another in love was rooted in the calling we have received. We weren't deserving of salvation before God called us, and neither are we deserving of salvation now. None of us have attained spiritual perfection. All of us deal with sinful drifting of various kinds. If we keep this in mind, then we will be able to lovingly accept other believers who are struggling to be like Jesus. Showing grace to others comes naturally when we realize that we fall short of the glory of God, when we realize that our only boast is in a Savior who has lifted us out of sin and reconciled us to God.

One of the ways we live worthy of the calling we have received is through gracious, truthful interaction with those inside and outside of the church community. Truth is not opposed to grace. We cannot have one without the other.

There's something else we need for unity, or better said, Someone else: God's Spirit (v. 3). The peace of God binds us together, yes. But this peace we have with fellow believers is not built upon a fragile agreement of cultural commonalities. No, our peace flows from being indwelled by the same Spirit.

We are one body united by the same Holy Spirit, who has called each of us to a common hope in salvation. We also have the same Lord, Jesus, with whom we have a relationship through saving faith. We have been identified with Him through the symbolic act of baptism. Because of His work on our behalf, we are adopted into the family of God.

Your church *is* united by faith in Jesus Christ. In this sense, unity is not something we strive to produce but something we strive to display before a watching world. You don't create unity. You live it out.

The outworking of our unity is the byproduct of the unified work of the Trinity in bringing about salvation. And one of the clearest demonstrations of the character of God is a unified body of believers identified by their love for one another in spite of their age, gender, race, sociological, or political differences (John 13:34-45).

The exercise of unity (Phil. 2:1-4)

The unity of the church can easily devolve into a utopian ideal that is not grounded in reality, especially if it is not established in truth and grace. Some would have us believe that we must focus solely upon grace to maintain unity. But this approach actually cheapens the grace that was provided through the work of Jesus and minimizes the hard truths of the gospel (sin, salvation, holiness, restoration). Others would have us focus solely upon truth to maintain unity. But this can turn the truth into a tool that demands complete uniformity while grace is offered only to those who are deemed worthy—a concept that flies in the face of the unearned nature of grace. Neither approach is true. Neither approach is gracious.

Thankfully, there is a better way to approach unity that does not pit truth and grace against one another. Unity can be sustained in the church when all of us work hard to overcome selfishness and pride by focusing upon something bigger than ourselves. This is the standard that Paul held up as the model for Christian unity—a unity that reflects the continuing work of the Holy Spirit in God's people.

1 *If then there is any encouragement in Christ, if any consolation of love, if any fellowship with the Spirit, if any affection and mercy,* 2 *fulfill my joy by thinking the same way, having the same love, sharing the same feelings, focusing on one goal.* 3 *Do nothing out of rivalry or conceit, but in humility consider others as more important than yourselves.* 4 *Everyone should look out not only for his own interests, but also for the interests of others.*

Paul called the Philippian church to fulfill his joy through being unified, and he provided a guide for preserving unity. He emphasized the intimacy of community. In a day when many people question the importance of belonging to a local church, we must remember it is impossible to achieve unity outside of consistent fellowship with believers in the church. It is hard to imagine the Philippians being like-minded if they never spent time together. This principle implies that active participation within a body of believers is essential to unity.

In the book (and subsequent films) *The Lord of the Rings*, a group composed of various races from Middle-earth is chosen to assist a lone hobbit, Frodo, in the destruction of a dangerous and powerful ring. This group is called the "fellowship of the ring," and over the course of the novels, the characters develop deep community. Though they come from various backgrounds and have different approaches to life, they experience unity through a common mission. They don't always get along, but the goal they share enables them to overcome numerous obstacles that arise in their journey.

Similarly, church unity flows from our focus upon the singular goal of fulfilling the Great Commission of Jesus in the world. Far too often we strive after biblical community when community is not the goal of the church. Community comes as the byproduct of sharing the mission of God. The mission is bigger than any one of us, which is why Paul stressed the need to refrain from rivalry and conceit. We are not competing against one another as though "lone ranger Christians" should accomplish the mission.

Churches will be most unified when Christians are consumed by something greater than themselves. Too many people join a church for the benefits they will receive. But few join a church for the way it seeks to benefit *others*. We must look out for the best interests of others if we are going to experience Spirit-given unity.

Humility is an essential element of holding fast to unity because it displays the sacrificial nature of Jesus that serves as the pattern for the Christian life and community. When unity is the result of a common goal, then believers will model Christlike humility through the power of the Spirit, and the message of the gospel will be powerfully and winsomely proclaimed to a lost world.

The example of unity (Philem. 15-18)

From his prison cell, the apostle Paul urged churches to pursue unity grounded in truth and marked by grace. He also provided a powerful example of what that unity looks like *on the ground*. His personal letter to Philemon was in reference to a slave, Onesimus, who had fled from Philemon's house. It is likely that Onesimus had stolen from Philemon and had cost his master more than the lost productivity of a laborer.

During his time away, Onesimus became a Christian through the witness of Paul, just as Paul had led Philemon to faith in Christ at an earlier occasion in his ministry. Philemon was an active participant in the Colossian church, and this personal letter is Paul's request of Philemon to receive Onesimus back into his home. Paul based his appeal on the transforming power of the gospel to unify a slave and his master as equal participants in the family of God.

15 *For perhaps this is why he was separated from you for a brief time, so that you might get him back permanently,* 16 *no longer as a slave, but more than a slave—as a dearly loved brother. He is especially so to me, but even more to you, both in the flesh and in the Lord.*

17 *So if you consider me a partner, accept him as you would me.* 18 *And if he has wronged you in any way, or owes you anything, charge that to my account.*

Notice the language that Paul used to describe Onesimus in this letter. He referred to him as a "dearly loved brother." This elevated him to a new level of relationship with Philemon. One of the most frequently used images for God's people is that of a family. Believers are called brothers and sisters, and God is referred to as our Father.

Family language permeates the New Testament, and when understood properly, it can help us see others in ways that transcend the cultural distinctions and divisions that can be barriers to unity. Paul emphasized this family connection of believers in his letter in order to convince Philemon of his responsibility to look upon his former slave as an heir to the kingdom of God.

Do you see how the burden of the relationship was primarily placed upon Philemon? But couldn't he protest that he was the one who was wronged? Yes, and that is Paul's point. The forgiveness we extend and the grace we show is rooted in the exchange that took place upon the cross.

Just like Onesimus, we too were slaves, but our enslavement was to the cruel master of sin. Our sin debt was a burden unable to be overcome by mere human effort or merit. It was precisely at this point that Jesus stepped in to pay the cost and free all who believe. Jesus put Himself in our place upon the cross for our sins, took our punishment upon Himself, and brought peace and unity with God. Theologians refer to this transaction as *substitutionary atonement*, the biblical teaching that harmony between God and man could only be accomplished through the substitution of the Righteous (Jesus) for the unrighteous (1 Pet. 3:18).

This truth provides the backdrop for Paul's resolution to the issue of Onesimus' return to Philemon. The rebellion of Onesimus demanded a response on Philemon's part. But Paul asked Philemon not to hold the debt against Onesimus. Rather, Paul emulated the Savior by substituting himself for Onesimus. He requested that any debt be placed on *his* account, and he asked Philemon to accept Onesimus in the same way that Paul had been accepted.

This is a very real application of how the truth of substitutionary atonement works in the life of the church. God looks at believers in the same way that He looks upon His own Son. We become His children by faith, and the penalty for our sin has been put on the account of the Son of God, who stood in our place and provided full and final payment for a debt He did not accrue. Paul modeled this when he stepped in the place of Onesimus and asked Philemon to seek unity instead of retribution.

Because grace and love are intimately linked together, people assume that love is non-confrontational. Not so. Love is intimately linked with truth, and it is the truth of God's love for fallen people that confronts us in our sin and graciously provides restoration.

In this letter Paul displayed the dynamic of confrontation motivated by love. Philemon was never forced to act according to Paul's desires. But Paul genuinely sought to motivate him to the action of accepting Onesimus as a *brother*, not merely a slave, which would highlight the continuing work of the gospel in Philemon's life.

Conclusion

Displaying unity is not the ultimate goal of the church, but it does reflect our commitment to the One who is ultimate. Demonstrating unity is a matter of obedience. We are to walk in a manner worthy of the calling we have received from God, a calling that includes humbly uniting together under the lordship of our God and Savior, Jesus.

The gospel unites us as followers of Jesus in spite of our differences. As a community of believers, the church should model the kingdom of God in the sight of the kingdoms of man. The church exists to declare good news to a divided world that King Jesus has risen and has the power to unite us under His banner. The world will recognize the nature of God's kingdom through our interactions with one another in the church. We must commit ourselves to lovingly share the truth and act as agents of God's grace within the church community and in the streets.

The gospel exalts Jesus and reminds us that outside of the grace of God, we too would have remained captives to sin. True unity can only be experienced through the glorious transformation that comes through Jesus' death, burial, and resurrection. The gospel shakes us from the trappings of a self-centered existence and gives us a grand purpose for living.

HYMN OF *Response*

The Church's one foundation Is Jesus Christ, her Lord;
She is His new creation, By Spirit and the Word;
From heav'n He came and sought her To be His holy bride;
With His own blood He bought her, And for her life He died.

Elect from ev'ry nation, Yet one o'er all the earth,
Her charter of salvation: One Lord, one faith, one birth;
One holy name she blesses, Partakes one holy food,
And to one hope she presses, With ev'ry grace endued.

'Mid toil and tribulation, And tumult of her war,
She waits the consummation Of peace forevermore;
Till with the vision glorious Her longing eyes are blest,
And the great Church victorious Shall be the Church at rest.
–Samuel J. Stone

Devotions

ONE BODY, MANY PARTS

Read 1 Corinthians 12:12-27.

Our bodies bear the unmistakable mark of God's diverse design. Though we have two hands and feet, they are divided into right and left for maximum capability. The hair in our ears and nose is not simply for added grooming as we get older. This seemingly insignificant hair provides protection from diseases that would make their way into our bodies through these access points without natural blockades. On an even smaller level, each part of our bodies is made up of thousands of microscopic cells. Even the slightest flaw in a cell can lead to various forms of cancer.

Just as the church is compared to a family, it is also compared to a body. There are various parts that make up the whole. Each part serves a role in the proper function of the body. Each member is interconnected with the other members, no matter how seemingly insignificant their role may be. As Paul wrote, "If one member suffers, all the members suffer with it." Imagine how your whole body reacts to pain, sickness, or emotional trauma.

We must take our responsibility to the body of Christ seriously and humbly. We must seek to remain unified for the health of the church. We also must learn how to appreciate the other members of the body. The diversity of the church should cause us to praise God's creativity and learn to humbly accept that we need others to walk alongside us as we carry out the mission God has given to us.

Pause and Reflect

1 Why is the body a good illustration of the church?

- -

2 How can you rejoice and suffer with other members of the body?

The Purpose of Forgiveness

Read Colossians 3:12-14.

The Hiding Place was written by Corrie ten Boom and tells the story of her family's assistance of Jews in Holland during World War II. After being caught, they were sent to a Nazi prison camp, Ravensbruck, where they were mistreated at the hands of the prison guards. Corrie was ultimately freed and later began speaking of her experience of the grace God displayed during and following her captivity.

At one such speaking engagement, Corrie came face-to-face with one of her former captors, a man she remembered for his brutality toward her and her sister. Her message had been on the forgiveness that God provided. At the end, he approached her and asked to be forgiven. He related that he had since become a Christian and was glad that God had forgiven him of his evil past. But he wanted to hear from a former prisoner that he had been forgiven. After a few moments of inner conflict, she made the choice to forgive the guard. She later testified, "I had never known God's love so intensely as I did then." [3]

Forgiveness can be difficult, but it is powerful. When we choose to forgive, we are reminded of the great act necessary to forgive us of the sins we have committed against God. God's purpose in commanding us to forgive is to remind us of the gospel of grace. We did not deserve and could not earn God's forgiveness, but He gave it nonetheless. When we look to the cross of Jesus and see the cost of forgiveness, our only response should be to forgive as we have been forgiven.

Pause and Reflect

1   Why is forgiveness difficult?

----

2   How can looking to the gospel change our perspective on forgiving others?

Whom Do You Represent?

Read Philippians 1:27-30; 1 Peter 2:11-17.

During my senior year of high school in Dallas, my dad became the pastor of a church in West Virginia. My parents graciously allowed me to stay with the family of a good friend while I finished my last semester. This was before the days of high-speed Internet and video chatting, so my mom regularly wrote me letters and sent pictures to update me on what was happening at our new home.

It was at this time that she began ending her letters and cards with a pattern that continues to this day. She always reminded me of whom I represent—our family, our church, the school I was attending, and our Savior, Jesus.

As I have taken on more responsibilities in life (marriage, children, jobs), the list has grown. However, the one constant has been the reminder that I am a representative of Jesus. When we become followers of Jesus, we bear His name before a watching world.

Being a follower of Christ has great responsibilities. The advent of social media has been both positive and negative for the reputation of God's people. On one hand, many believers have effectively used these sites as tools for spreading the gospel. However, many have used them to proclaim opposing messages. Under religion they may put "Christian," but their posts communicate something wholly different.

God has entrusted us not only with His message but also with His name. We are the greatest evidence of His gospel's power to transform sinners. Represent Him well.

Pause and Reflect

1   What are some ways that we represent God in our world?

- -

2   What area of your life sends mixed signals about your commitment to Christ?

DISCUSSION QUESTIONS

1 Have you or someone you know been part of a church that split? What are some things churches tend to divide over? How do our divisions affect our witness? What would you do in a church situation if many in the congregation were explicitly denying core Christian doctrines?

2 What reasons might Paul have had for emphasizing the word "one" in Ephesians 4:4-6? In what ways does the church's unity reflect the character of God?

3 Put yourself in Paul's chains. If you were writing from prison to Christians you knew and loved, what would you want them to know? What would your focus be?

4 Why do Christians often feel a tension between grace and truth? How does the truthfulness of Scripture cause us to rethink what "love" is and what "loving" looks like?

5 What are some examples of unity that come about as the result of a shared mission? The church is to be active in the mission of God together, not just as individuals. How can a church corporately fulfill the mission?

6 In what ways does our congregation look out for the interests of others—believers and unbelievers?

7 Is unity the same thing as uniformity? How can Christians in church learn to disagree well?

8 Discuss ways the church is like a family. In what ways does this truth show our common salvation in Christ as well as the sense of permanence we share in our relationships with one other?

9 How does Paul ground the unity of Philemon and Onesimus in the gospel? What can the Letter to Philemon teach us about the necessity of confrontation with those we love?

10 How does the vision of love in Philemon counter the definitions and expressions of "love" we see in the world?

Part 3

LIVING IN LIGHT OF THE RETURNING KING

Because of Jesus' saving work, believers are justified before God, united to Christ and declared righteous. This salvation frees Christians to serve the living God from gratitude rather than fear. The Father shepherds His people through pastors and His Word. Though temptations and trials come, God preserves His people in faith for the day when the King returns to set things right and to dwell with His people for all eternity.

Chapter 10

Justification

The King Declares Guilty People Righteous

VOICES FROM *Church History*

"The utility of the law may be shown by this, that it obliges all whom it proves guilty of transgression to betake themselves to grace for deliverance...For it rather commands than assists; it discovers disease, but does not heal it; nay, the malady that is not healed is rather aggravated by it, so that the cure of grace is more earnestly and anxiously sought for." [1]

–Augustine (354-430)

VOICES FROM *the Church*

"Saving faith is a commitment to Jesus as Savior and Lord. It is a personal and individual decision. It is more than assent to historical or theological truth given to us in God's Word. It is faith in the promises of God that all who trust in Christ will not perish but have eternal life." [2]

–Billy Graham

In the 1998 movie *Saving Private Ryan*, a group of U.S. soldiers are sent on a rescue mission behind enemy lines to retrieve a paratrooper, James Ryan, who has lost three brothers in the second World War. Throughout their mission, several of these soldiers lose their lives. At the end of their mission, they find themselves in a heated battle where the captain of this group is critically injured. As American planes come to the rescue, Captain Miller pulls Ryan close and whispers his dying words: "Earn this." The movie ends with Ryan as an old man standing before his captain's gravesite, saying, "I hope that, at least in your eyes, I've earned what all of you have done for me."

Many people are familiar with the Bible's teaching that Jesus Christ has paid the ultimate sacrifice for us by dying on the cross for our sins. But we often fail to understand the proper response to this sacrifice. It is easy for people to assume that the call of Christianity is to acknowledge Christ's death for our sin and yet still think we must somehow earn what that sacrifice accomplished. Like the captain from Saving Private Ryan, Jesus also had some last words as He was dying. His last words were not "Earn this" but rather "It is finished!"

In this chapter, we will look at the apostle Paul's Letter to the Romans as well as a section from the Letter to the Hebrews. In these letters, we learn that justification is an act of God's free grace, in which He pardons all our sins and accepts us as righteous in His sight because the righteousness of Christ has been credited to us. By faith alone in Christ's sacrifice, believers are united to Christ and freed from slavery to sin to serve the living God.

All people are sinners, born "in Adam" and therefore guilty before God (Rom. 5:12-14).

12 *Therefore, just as sin entered the world through one man, and death through sin, in this way death spread to all men, because all sinned.* 13 *In fact, sin was in the world before the law, but sin is not charged to a person's account when there is no law.* 14 *Nevertheless, death reigned from Adam to Moses, even over those who did not sin in the likeness of Adam's transgression. He is a prototype of the Coming One.*

To understand the doctrine of justification, we need to set it within the story line of the Scriptures. Let's go back to the opening scene of the Bible. Adam and Eve (the first humans) had a perfect relationship with God in the garden of Eden until they listened to the serpent and chose to disobey God's command. In this story, we see sin for what it is—a deliberate and willful offense of disobedience against a holy God. Adam and Eve chose to trust in themselves rather than in the God who made them.

Through Adam, not only did sin come into the world, but death came as well. Sin earns death (Rom. 6:23). Because of their disobedience, Adam and Eve had a broken relationship with God, and therefore, they received the consequence of their sin—death. Since then, sin and death have spread to all human beings who are the descendants of Adam.

But God did not give up on His creation. After promising to send a Savior (Gen. 3:15), He blessed the family of Abraham and rescued them from slavery in Egypt. Then He gave them the law through His servant Moses. The passage we read in Romans 5 shows us the purpose of the law given to Moses. Though sin and death came into the world through Adam, the law allowed for sin to be "charged," or "counted." This means that the law came to show us our problem, that we are in fact sinners.

The law is like a carpenter's level. This tool is used to show a carpenter whether or not the foundation of a building is level. It can diagnose a problem but cannot fix it. The law "confines" us by showing us we are sinners. It was not meant to be a means to achieve righteousness but a mirror to reflect our sinful nature and our need for salvation. It was to be a tutor to drive us to Jesus. The law shows us God's standard and that none of us can live up to it.

Do you see how Paul described our condition before coming to Christ? We are not sick in our sins but dead. If we were merely sick, then that suggests that we could do something about it. We might seek a doctor or medicine or therapy. But since we are dead in our sins, we need to be made alive with Christ. Jesus did not come just to make sick people healthy or bad people good, He came to make dead people *alive.*

Not only does sin bring forth death, but it also gives us a destiny. Romans 2:5 says, "But because of your hardness and unrepentant heart you are storing up wrath for yourself in the day of wrath, when God's righteous judgment is revealed." God is holy and just, and in His justice He must punish sin. Apart from Christ, all mankind is headed toward the wrath of God and eternal separation from God. But God's Word says that He sent His Son in order that the world might be saved through Him (John 3:17). Jesus did not come into a neutral world but a world full of sinners in rebellion against Him— sinners who are spiritually dead and destined for God's wrath. And Jesus is God's solution to our sin problem.

Those who trust in Jesus are reborn "in Christ" and declared righteous before God (Rom. 5:15-21; 8:1-2).

15 *But the gift is not like the trespass. For if by the one man's trespass the many died, how much more have the grace of God and the gift overflowed to the many by the grace of the one man, Jesus Christ.* 16 *And the gift is not like the one man's sin, because from one sin came the judgment, resulting in condemnation, but from many trespasses came the gift, resulting in justification.* 17 *Since by the one man's trespass, death reigned through that one man, how much more will those who receive the overflow of grace and the gift of righteousness reign in life through the one man, Jesus Christ.*

18 *So then, as through one trespass there is condemnation for everyone, so also through one righteous act there is life-giving justification for everyone.* 19 *For just as through one man's disobedience the many were made sinners, so also through the one man's obedience the many will be made righteous.* 20 *The law came along to multiply the trespass. But where sin multiplied, grace multiplied even more* 21 *so that, just as sin reigned in death, so also grace will reign through righteousness, resulting in eternal life through Jesus Christ our Lord.*

Throughout the Old Testament story line, we see stories that testify and point forward to God providing the ultimate sacrifice through Jesus to save us from the penalty of sin. The Bible says that when Adam and Eve sinned, they knew they were naked and felt their shame. God then made them garments of animal skin and clothed them (Gen. 3). From the beginning, we see a picture of God moving to cover the sin and shame of mankind.

Years later, God called Abraham to offer his son Isaac as a sacrifice on top of a mountain in the land of Moriah (Gen. 22). Yet God provided a ram whose horns were caught in a thicket to take the place of Isaac on the altar of sacrifice. Isaac was restored to his father only because God provided a sacrifice in his place. Abraham called the place "Yahweh-yireh," which means "the LORD will provide."

In the story of the exodus, God led His people out of slavery in Egypt. He called for the people to put the blood of the Passover sacrifice on the doorposts of their houses. God declared that He would pass over the houses with blood on the doorposts when He passed through the land of Egypt to strike down the firstborn sons.

In the days of the tabernacle, God appointed a high priest from among His people who would be a mediator between the people and Himself. Once a year, this high priest offered the blood of a sacrifice in the most holy place for his sins and the sins of the people. This was an imperfect sacrifice that needed to be repeated every year.

These stories and rituals were intended to point forward to what this passage in Romans is all about—God's perfect, spotless sacrifice in the work of Jesus Christ. Jesus is God's grace in action. Jesus is God coming as a man to accomplish our salvation.

What is our appropriate response to Christ's sacrifice? Is God calling us to earn what He has done in the same way Captain Miller spoke to Private Ryan? Not at all. In Romans 5, Paul wrote that just as we were born sinners *in Adam*, it is our position in relation to Jesus and His work that makes us righteous. All people are either *in Adam* still or have moved to a position of being *in Christ*. And the only way to stand righteous before a holy God is to be found *in Christ*. Those of us who are *in Christ* receive a wonderful promise in Romans 8.

1 *Therefore, no condemnation now exists for those in Christ Jesus,* 2 *because the Spirit's law of life in Christ Jesus has set you free from the law of sin and of death.*

Remember once again the scene from the garden where Adam and Eve first sinned. They were naked and full of shame. There was no way to hide their sin. But God clothed them with garments made from animal skin. This is most likely a reference to the first sacrifice accepted by God. To say that men are still in Adam apart from Christ means that we are still dead in our sin. We are naked and need to be clothed with a sacrifice for our sins. Jesus is God's sacrifice that He has made to clothe us in righteousness.

This is referred to as "the Great Exchange." Jesus exchanges His righteousness with us for our sins. At the cross, our sins are imputed over to Jesus and He bears the wrath of God. In turn, through faith in Jesus, His righteousness is credited to our account. When people put their faith and trust in Christ and His work alone, they are declared righteous before a holy God. They are clothed in Christ's righteousness. They have moved by faith into the position of being *in Christ*.

Grace is the work of God to secure our salvation. Faith is the appropriate response to receive salvation. The idea of earning salvation is an affront to a gracious God. When someone is presented with a gift, it would be insulting to even try to pay for it. In regards to salvation, God has done the work through Jesus and is presenting it to the world as a gift. The only God-honoring response is to humbly receive it by faith. Any attempt to earn it can only be seen as a rejection of God's grace gift. So by grace, we must also come to the end of ourselves and receive by faith the gift of grace in Jesus.

The truth of justification (being "declared righteous") is related to the truth of sanctification (being "made righteous"). God's goal in salvation is not just to declare us righteous but to see us actually become holy and righteous as we are progressively set free from the remaining sin in our lives.

Marriage provides a picture of growing in love for God. Think of a man who pursues a woman romantically. He may take her on extravagant dates, buy her gifts, write her love letters, etc. Once they get married, they are "one flesh." But this should be the beginning—not the end—of their pursuing love for one another. For the rest of their lives, the husband and wife ought to pursue one another in love, growing in the oneness declared at their wedding ceremony.

Likewise, the moment we receive Christ, we are justified—declared righteous. And now by the grace of God and the work of the Holy Spirit, we are being sanctified—made righteous. The newborn Christian, grateful for grace and overflowing in love, pursues Jesus daily and slowly grows into His likeness.

Salvation by grace alone frees us to serve the living God (Heb. 9:11-14).

11 *But the Messiah has appeared, high priest of the good things that have come. In the greater and more perfect tabernacle not made with hands (that is, not of this creation),* 12 *He entered the most holy place once for all, not by the blood of goats and calves, but by His own blood, having obtained eternal redemption.* 13 *For if the blood of goats and bulls and the ashes of a young cow, sprinkling those who are defiled, sanctify for the purification of the flesh,* 14 *how much more will the blood of the Messiah, who through the eternal Spirit offered Himself without blemish to God, cleanse our consciences from dead works to serve the living God?*

Many wrongly believe that grace frees us up to do whatever sin we want. But this is a faulty view of grace. Grace is the unmerited favor of God given to us through the gift of Jesus' death and resurrection. It is a free gift, but it is a costly and saving gift. If someone receives a free shirt to add to his closet that is already full of shirts, he will have minimal gratitude. But if someone freely receives the cure to a rare deadly disease that he has, and it cost the giver everything he has, then he would give his life in service to the giver.

We've already seen how Jesus is the perfect sacrifice who "offered Himself without blemish to God" for our sins. This text tells us that Christ's sacrifice does not need to be repeated. Notice the last verse in this passage. Because of the perfect work of Christ, those who receive Him by faith are no longer slaves to sin and to dead works. In other words, since we have received the forgiveness of sins, Christians no longer need to work for it.

This is the major difference between Christianity and works-based religions. Only through the grace of God can one sincerely serve Him. In a works-based system, people are not truly serving God but themselves. Why? Because they are trying to achieve something for themselves. They are doing good works in order to receive salvation and forgiveness.

But grace removes the burden of trying to earn salvation. Grace frees us to serve God for Him alone. It's not that a Christian no longer does good works in service to God, but grace changes the motive.

In a works-based system, the motive to live for God is the fear of not being good enough for God and facing the consequences. In a grace-based system, the motive is not fear but love. Because you have already received the favor of God, your works are done as an expression of love for God. Good works are not the means to salvation but the proof of salvation. Since Christ served us in death, we are freed up to serve Him in life.

The truth of salvation by grace alone is also the fuel that drives us to serve God on His mission. The Bible teaches that those who have been brought into a right relationship with God through Jesus are now the means by which God draws others to Himself. In 2 Corinthians 5:18-19, Paul wrote: "Everything is from God, who reconciled us to Himself through Christ and gave us the ministry of reconciliation: That is, in Christ, God was reconciling the world to Himself, not counting their trespasses against them, and He has committed the message of reconciliation to us."

As Christians remember the grace they have received, they will be driven to serve God in this mission. Our compassion for others who do not know Christ wells up in our hearts as we remember our own situation before Christ entered our lives. When we call to mind the fact that we were separated from God and hopelessly dead in our own sins, our sense of entitlement wanes and our sympathy for others who need the same hope begins to grow.

Conclusion

Private Ryan stood with his wife and family at the gravesite of his fallen captain, hoping his life earned the sacrifice of his leader. It was the end of his own life, and his thoughts were gripped with a need to validate his choices.

The apostle Paul faced a similar moment at the end of his life. However, Paul understood that he did not need to earn what Christ had done for him. He understood that God is most honored when we simply receive His gift of grace by faith. Paul stated his life response to Christ's sacrifice by saying, "For I am already being poured out as a drink offering, and the time for my departure is close. I have fought the good fight, I have finished the race, I have kept the faith" (2 Tim. 4:6-7).

This is the Christian life. We cannot and must not attempt to earn what Christ has done for us. He is the sacrifice that is to be humbly received. When sinners receive this gift of grace, King Jesus declares them righteous before a holy God. They are now set free to live for God out of gratitude and love. We must now live our life as a drink offering wholly pleasing to Him. The goal of this life is that when people look at us, they do not see us, but they only see Jesus, the hope of this world!

- -

PRAYER OF *Response*

"Christ was all anguish that I might be all joy, cast off that I might be brought in, trodden down as an enemy that I might be welcomed as a friend, surrendered to hell's worst that I might attain heaven's best, stripped that I might be clothed, wounded that I might be healed, athirst that I might drink, tormented that I might be comforted, made a shame that I might inherit glory, entered darkness that I might have eternal light, My Savior wept that all tears might be wiped from my eyes, groaned that I might have endless song, endured all pain that I might have unfading health, bore a thorned crown that I might have a glory-diadem, bowed his head that I might uplift mine, experienced reproach that I might receive welcome, closed his eyes in death that I might gaze on unclouded brightness, expired that I might for ever live…Go forth, O conquering God, and show me the cross, mighty to subdue, comfort and save."[3]

–Puritan prayer

Devotions

GOOD ENOUGH?

Ephesians 2:8-9: "For you are saved by grace through faith, and this is not from yourselves; it is God's gift—not from works, so that no one can boast."

Growing up as a Muslim, I was taught that during my life two angels were recording all of my good and bad deeds. I was told that at the Day of Judgment before God, all of my good and bad works would be weighed against each other upon a scale. If I had more good in my life, I was going to paradise. If I had more bad deeds, then I was going to hell.

The problem with this thinking, of course, is that it has a faulty view of God's standard and therefore misdiagnoses our problem. It assumes that through our own efforts we can attain a level of "good enough" before God. But what is God's standard of good? Is it 51 percent? Since Scripture teaches us that God is holy, righteous, and perfect, wouldn't His standard be 100 percent? And if His standard is perfection, wouldn't that be unattainable for us?

That's why the Christian gospel is good news. Jesus accomplished our salvation by His perfect life and death. If we receive His gift through repentance and faith, we are saved by His grace. There is assurance. If we are saved by the "scale system" of works, can we ever have assurance?

Some confuse assurance with arrogance. They believe it's arrogant to know for sure you will be in heaven. But it depends on whose work you are trusting in. It would be extremely arrogant for me to say I know I will be in heaven based on what I have done. But arrogance is removed when I say I know I will be in heaven based on what Christ has done for me. Whom are you trusting?

Pause and Reflect

1   What are some ways you are trusting in your own works for God's favor?

- -

2   Is your life marked by assurance in Christ, or is there an undercurrent of unrest?

Transforming Grace

2 Corinthians 4:15: "Indeed, everything is for your benefit, so that grace, extended through more and more people, may cause thanksgiving to increase to God's glory."

Did you know there is a direct link between grace and thanksgiving? According to this verse, thanksgiving arises in our hearts from a proper understanding of the grace we have been given by God. We are justified before God because of the death of His Son, Jesus, to pay for our sins.

If our justification is of our own effort, then there is no thanksgiving because it would be seen as something we deserve. But when our hearts embrace grace, gratitude extends toward God, and therefore, God is glorified in our lives. A thankful heart is a worshiping heart.

Grace also has an overflowing effect in the hearts of believers. As it is received, it is extended toward others. Philippians 2 says we are to count others as more significant than ourselves and to consider the interests of others as well as our own. Paul pointed to the example of Jesus—though equal with God, He put His rights aside, came into our world, and died for our sins. This is even more astounding when we realize that we were in rebellion against God as His enemies. Yet God still extended grace toward us.

This grace changes the way we view all relationships. If we have received this kind of love, we are likewise to put our rights aside and extend grace toward others, even if they don't deserve it. These relationships are an opportunity for us to glorify God by mimicking His heart of grace.

Pause and Reflect

1   Spend time worshiping God by expressing your thanks for His grace.

- -

2   Who are some people in your life you find it difficult to extend grace toward?

- -

3   How does God's love for you in Christ help you extend grace toward others?

THE SENDING GOSPEL

Take a look at John 17:18-20; 20:21 and you'll see that the gospel results in people being sent. Just as Jesus was sent into the world to save us, we are sent into the world with His Word so others might believe in Him. His mission does not terminate with us but rather continues through us.

It is important to remember why Jesus has left us in this world. He has not left us here only to pursue a career, marriage, and family. These are great things, but we should see them as avenues to fulfill our greatest mission.

People often identify themselves by their careers. When we think of a Christian doctor, we think of a doctor who happens to be a Christian. But how would we live life differently if, instead, we thought of a Christian doctor as an ambassador for Christ who is fulfilling that mission through his medical practice? With an eternal perspective, we see every arena we are placed in as a mission field.

As ambassadors, we are to proclaim the gospel in word and deed. In 1 Corinthians 9, Paul said that he served all men in order to win more to Christ. Just as Christ came not to be served but to serve and to give His life as a ransom, we are to be the hands and feet of Christ by serving those who do not know Him. But we are also to share the gospel through word. An ambassador is sent to a foreign land to speak on behalf of his leader. We are declared righteous by Jesus so that we might declare His righteousness to the world.

Pause and Reflect

1   Into what arenas of the world has Christ sent you to fulfill His mission?

- -

2   What are some ways you can proclaim the gospel with your words and demonstrate it with your deeds?

Discussion Questions

1   What is the difference between the response of Private Ryan to his captain's sacrifice and the response of the Christian to Christ's sacrifice?

----

2   What is it about human nature that causes us to try to "earn" the rewards that come from Christ's sacrifice?

----

3   What are the signs in the world around us that sin and death have spread to all mankind since the fall of Adam?

----

4   Why is sin related to death? What are the consequences of sin in the relationships between people?

----

5   How does the severity of the law's diagnosis of sin drive us to the cross? How does the understanding that we are spiritually dead apart from Christ affect our prayers for those who do not know Him?

----

6   What are some examples from the Old Testament that point forward to the future sufficient sacrifice of Christ on the cross as a payment for the sins of mankind?

----

7   How does your view of God change when you consider the fact that God's Son became a man not only to be our mediator but also our sacrifice? How does this truth differ from other religions?

----

8   Why was Christ's sacrifice permanent and effective? How does our service to the King demonstrate our faith in Christ's atonement?

----

9   What are some problems with confusing justification (being "declared righteous") and sanctification (being "made righteous")? What motivates your obedience: gratitude for Christ's work or lingering guilt and fear?

----

10   How does your understanding of the gospel impact your perspective on living out the Christian life?

Chapter 11

Following

The King Shepherds His People

"See that the work of saving grace be thoroughly wrought in your own souls…Take heed to yourselves, lest you perish, while you call upon others to take heed of perishing; and lest you famish yourselves while you prepare food for them." [1]
–Richard Baxter (1615-1691)

"When the work of shepherding is difficult, the commitment of the shepherd is truly revealed. Yet shepherding is a labor of love to the one who truly is a shepherd." [2]
–Timothy Witmer

"The LORD is my shepherd." Have you ever stopped to think about these famous words from King David in Psalm 23? How they shape our understanding of our relationship with God?

Throughout the Old Testament, we see God guiding, protecting, leading, and restoring His people—just like a shepherd with his sheep. Then in the New Testament, we see Jesus declaring Himself to be the "Good Shepherd" and commanding one of His disciples, Peter, to tend and feed His sheep. Years later, this same Peter would exhort the leaders of the churches scattered throughout Asia Minor to "shepherd God's flock among you" (1 Pet. 5:2).

From the words written by a shepherd named David in Psalm 23 to the ministry of Jesus and His disciples, it is clear that God has always intended for His people to be shepherded. God's primary way of shepherding His people is through called and gifted pastors who serve under the authority of King Jesus, the Good Shepherd.

Near the end of his life, the apostle Paul wrote letters to Timothy and Titus, two of his most trusted children in the faith, instructing them in their efforts to model the Good Shepherd, who guides His people into the knowledge of truth. In these letters, we learn much about what is expected from our pastors today. We also learn how to pray for and support these pastors given to us by God to lead us.

Shepherds serve God's people by embodying the truth they proclaim (1 Tim. 4:11-16).

In his first letter to Timothy, Paul exhorted this young disciple to walk closely with Jesus Christ, the chief Shepherd, and to lead the church as Christ would have him to. In 1 Timothy 4:11-16, Paul wrote:

11 *Command and teach these things.* 12 *Let no one despise your youth; instead, you should be an example to the believers in speech, in conduct, in love, in faith, in purity.* 13 *Until I come, give your attention to public reading, exhortation, and teaching.* 14 *Do not neglect the gift that is in you; it was given to you through prophecy, with the laying on of hands by the council of elders.* 15 *Practice these things; be committed to them, so that your progress may be evident to all.* 16 *Pay close attention to your life and your teaching; persevere in these things, for by doing this you will save both yourself and your hearers.*

Pastors are expected to live according to the teaching they proclaim. Do you see how Paul exhorted Timothy to practice what he preached (v. 15)? And to pay attention to his own life (v. 16)?

In the Old Testament, you find this principle throughout the history of Israel. Though God was King and Shepherd over Israel, the people begged Samuel the prophet for a human king to be like the other nations. After the disastrous reign of Saul, who didn't live according to God's commands, God told Samuel that He would choose one of Jesse's sons to be the next king.

When Samuel visited Jesse's home, he met all of Jesse's sons except one, David, because he was shepherding the flock his father had entrusted to him. No doubt all of David's brothers wanted to be the next king to shepherd the people of Israel. But David was the only one who was actually living out his calling as a shepherd. And God, the Shepherd King, bypassed all of the brothers and selected the shepherd boy, David, to be king of Israel.

Scripture teaches that one who is faithful in little will also be faithful in much (Luke 16:10). David was faithful with the little sheep first, and God put him over the people of Israel later.

Paul also taught Timothy that he should show progress in leading an exemplary life and that this progress should be evident to all (v. 15). It may seem, at first, that Paul was endorsing an arrogant, self-righteous showiness. But the word translated "progress" was used in military circles to describe an advancing force that would go out before the rest of the army and clear any obstacles that would hinder the rest of the troops.

In this light, we see that a pastor's exemplary life ought to clear out a path toward righteousness for others to follow. The shepherd's life should not hinder spiritual growth for others but help promote it. Far from being a call to arrogance, this is about laying one's desires aside and pursuing righteousness for the betterment of the flock.

Paul stressed to Timothy that no one should despise his youth. In his selfless courage on behalf of his people, Timothy must take the initiative and set an example for other believers to follow both in word and deed. Paul encouraged others to imitate him just as he imitated Christ (1 Cor. 11:1). In the same way, the pastor's example must so closely mirror Christ's that if anyone were to imitate the pastor, they would essentially be imitating Christ.

Paul challenged Timothy to "persevere" in embodying the truth he proclaimed, "for by doing this you will save both yourself and your hearers" (1 Tim. 4:16). The gospel goes forward as it is communicated through the pastor's teaching and demonstrated through the pastor's life.

Consider the contrast between two biblical characters—Noah and Lot. Noah walked with God as a righteous man, blameless in his generation (Gen. 6:9). He obeyed God when he was called to build the ark, and he did this "to deliver his family" (Heb. 11:7). Noah lived according to his faith in God's word about the coming flood. Noah's family was so influenced by his faith that they went on board and were saved when the flood came.

On the other hand, Lot did not live out his faith before his family. He chose to live in a city given over to sin and wickedness, and instead of influencing the city for good, Lot blended in. When Lot warned his family about God's judgment, they responded as if he were "joking" (Gen. 19:14). Because Lot had not displayed a righteous life before his family, his words had no power with them.

How we live matters. That's why Paul urged Timothy to pay careful attention not only to his teaching but also to his life. Pastors must be known for sound doctrine (orthodoxy) and sound living (orthopraxy) because both play a significant role in the shepherding of God's people.

Shepherds serve God's people by preaching truth, even when it is costly (2 Tim. 4:1-8).

1 *I solemnly charge you before God and Christ Jesus, who is going to judge the living and the dead, and because of His appearing and His kingdom:* 2 *Proclaim the message; persist in it whether convenient or not; rebuke, correct, and encourage with great patience and teaching.* 3 *For the time will come when they will not tolerate sound doctrine, but according to their own desires, will multiply teachers for themselves because they have an itch to hear something new.* 4 *They will turn away from hearing the truth and will turn aside to myths.* 5 *But as for you, be serious about everything, endure hardship, do the work of an evangelist, fulfill your ministry.*

6 *For I am already being poured out as a drink offering, and the time for my departure is close.* 7 *I have fought the good fight, I have finished the race, I have kept the faith.* 8 *There is reserved for me in the future the crown of righteousness, which the Lord, the righteous Judge, will give me on that day, and not only to me, but to all those who have loved His appearing.*

In his first letter to Timothy, Paul discussed how one should behave in the household of God. He stated that the church is the pillar and foundation of the truth (1 Tim. 3:15). As the pillar, the church is to uphold and proclaim sound doctrine. As the foundation, the church is to defend the truth against false doctrine. Elders in the church must be able to give instruction in sound doctrine and also to rebuke those who contradict it (Titus 1:9). What is the source of sound doctrine? The Bible declares about itself that it is breathed out by God and profitable for doctrine (2 Tim. 3:16). As such, the Bible is the authority over all our lives. The health of a church is in large part due to the overall view of the authority of Scripture—from the shepherds to the sheep. A healthy church is one where its members submit themselves to the Word of God over their own passions.

Throughout Scripture, we see that the effectiveness of shepherds is measured by how they place the needs of the sheep above their own. For example, in Ezekiel 34, the Lord rebuked the shepherds of Israel because they clothed and fed themselves to the neglect of God's sheep. Because of the shepherds' failure to tend to the people, God promised to come Himself as the Shepherd.

The Jewish leaders of Jesus' day also showed themselves to be poor shepherds. It's interesting to see how, after Jesus raised a dead man to life, the priests and Pharisees were worried that the Romans would come and take away their authority (John 11:48). They were so concerned about losing their positions of authority that they overlooked the fact that someone was raised from the dead! Again, these leaders were more worried about themselves than the sheep.

In John 10, Jesus distinguished Himself as the Good Shepherd, not the hired hand who sees a wolf coming and abandons the sheep. Jesus is the Good Shepherd who lays down His life for the sheep.

It's no wonder that when Peter instructed the elders in the churches of Asia Minor, he called them to shepherd the flock "according to God's will; not for the money but eagerly; not lording it over those entrusted to you, but being examples to the flock" (1 Pet. 5:2-3). As shepherds of the church, pastors should model the selfless attitude of Jesus, the chief Shepherd. He put the interests of the church before His own when He embraced the plan of God by dying on the cross for the sins of mankind.

Paul also prepared Timothy for hardship as a pastor by telling him that some in the church would not tolerate sound doctrine. People would turn toward teaching that suits their passions. Nevertheless, Timothy's message was to remain the same.

It is important for us to pray for our pastors that they would choose to please Christ over man (Gal. 1:10). If pastors are only interested in their own welfare, then they will choose to avoid the calling of proclaiming sound doctrine when it is unpopular. But if pastors are motivated by love for the sheep and what is best for the flock, then they will uphold the truth even when it is inconvenient.

Pastors must preach the truth, even when it is costly or when people turn away. Why? Because it is a sign of true love for the sheep and genuine concern for the health of the flock.

God's people follow the shepherd by submitting to God's Word (Titus 2:11-14).

Just as pastors are to embody and proclaim sound doctrine, the sheep (God's people) must also live according to God's truth. Take a look at this passage from Paul's letter to Titus:

11 *For the grace of God has appeared with salvation for all people,* 12 *instructing us to deny godlessness and worldly lusts and to live in a sensible, righteous, and godly way in the present age,* 13 *while we wait for the blessed hope and appearing of the glory of our great God and Savior, Jesus Christ.* 14 *He gave Himself for us to redeem us from all lawlessness and to cleanse for Himself a people for His own possession, eager to do good works.*

Christians are God's sheep. We follow the chief Shepherd, Jesus, by obeying His Word and submitting to the loving authority of the shepherds (pastors) God has placed over us. Of course, it's not just church leaders who must embody the truth of the gospel in their lives. We are all called to obedience.

The passage above shows that Christ gave up His life to redeem us from lawlessness, to make us His people, and to free us to do good works for His glory. Through faith in Jesus Christ, we are not only forgiven of our sins, but God also adopts us as His children and leads us into a life marked by righteousness.

Just as we saw a distinction between true and false shepherds, we also see in God's Word a distinction made between true and false sheep. *False sheep* are wolves in sheep's clothing, recognized by their actions, which are not in line with the Scriptures (Matt. 7:15-20). *True sheep* know the voice of the Shepherd and follow Him. They reject the voice of strangers (John 10:4-5).

As Christians, we follow Jesus by submitting to God's word. Through time spent with the Lord in His Word, we come to know His voice. We can distinguish it from other voices that lead people astray. As we follow the voice of Jesus, we are empowered to deny godlessness and live in an upright way. Though we are not completely free from sin's presence, our lives should be marked by growth in righteousness as we follow the Shepherd.

Paul also instructed Titus on the eternal perspective God's people should have as we pursue godly lives. Our pursuit of righteousness is spurred on by our waiting for the appearing of our "great God and Savior, Jesus Christ." When He appears, we will be ushered out of lawlessness and into a world free from sin, a world marked by the physical presence of the Good Shepherd. Until that day, we are to strive to live in a way that reflects our future hope.

Our deeds either confirm or deny our faith. Abraham Lincoln's supporters represented him at his party's nominating convention for the 1860 presidential election. They endeavored to conduct themselves in such a way that they gave no offense to anyone as they spoke with delegations, "taking them in detail and making no fuss." Believing that people had already made up their mind about who their first choice in the election would be, these supporters sought to make Lincoln the second choice of delegations, if not their first choice. [3] As rounds of ballots were cast, people's first choice fell to the wayside; these people then turned to Lincoln. He won the nomination and eventually the presidency.

As followers of Christ, our actions should declare to the world a better way of living. Our hope is that when people's worldly pursuits fail them, they will find hope in Jesus Christ and follow the Good Shepherd.

The sheep also follow the Shepherd by engaging in the mission of the Shepherd. The Shepherd is pursuing a "people for His own possession." After Jesus revealed Himself to be the Good Shepherd who lays down His life for the sheep, He went on to say: "But I have other sheep that are not of this fold; I must bring them also, and they will listen to My voice. Then there will be one flock, one shepherd" (John 10:16).

The work of salvation that God started in us was not intended to end with us. It goes out to other "sheep." We serve a Shepherd on mission to save lost sheep. What's astonishing is that God has chosen to use us as His ambassadors to accomplish this mission!

Jesus emptied Himself, took the form of a servant, and became obedient to the point of death to save us. In order to participate in this mission of God, we too must leave behind our comforts and go after those who have not yet been reconciled to Him. We must push aside our selfish desires and join God in His mission of bringing back lost sheep!

Conclusion

The Bible often speaks of the Shepherd/sheep relationship between God and His people. God is the One who seeks the lost sheep, heals their wounds, restores them, feeds them, and guides them.

"The LORD is my shepherd; there is nothing I lack. He lets me lie down in green pastures; He leads me beside quiet waters. He renews my life; He leads me along the right paths for His name's sake." These famous verses from Psalm 23 have long shaped the way every devout Jew views their relationship to God. The Hebrew people were God's chosen people, and they saw God as their Shepherd and themselves as "the sheep of His pasture" (Ps. 100:3). God has always been the One guiding, protecting, leading, and restoring them.

This is why it was so revolutionary when Jesus said to the Jews of His day that He was the Good Shepherd who knows His own sheep, goes before them, and leads them (see John 10). The Jews correctly understood this statement as a declaration of the deity of Jesus. Jesus is the living God who came into this world to lead and shepherd His people. As the Good Shepherd, He would eventually lay His life down for His sheep.

The Word of God teaches us that we are like sheep and have all gone astray (Isa. 53:6). God ultimately sought us through the Son, Jesus Christ. Jesus is our Good Shepherd who loves and leads us.

Jesus shepherds His people through pastors of the flock. We must pray for our pastors to be true to their calling as shepherds, to selflessly and courageously lead people into truth. As members of the church, we follow Jesus and His Word above all, and we pray for and submit to the leaders in our church as they guide us.

PRAYER OF *Response*

"Lord God, You have appointed me as a Bishop and Pastor in Your Church, but you see how unsuited I am to meet so great and difficult a task. If I had lacked Your help, I would have ruined everything long ago. Therefore, I call upon You: I wish to devote my mouth and my heart to you; I shall teach the people. I myself will learn and ponder diligently upon Your Word. Use me as Your instrument—but do not forsake me, for if ever I should be on my own, I would easily wreck it all."[4]

–Martin Luther

Devotions

THE LORD IS MY SHEPHERD

Psalm 23:4: "Even when I go through the darkest valley, I fear no danger, for You are with me; Your rod and Your staff—they comfort me."

Throughout the Old Testament, God is portrayed as a loving shepherd who guides, protects, restores, and feeds his sheep (His people). This shepherd-sheep relationship is reinforced in the New Testament. Jesus reveals Himself to be the Good Shepherd, and those who follow Him are His sheep.

In Psalm 23, the tools the Shepherd uses to lead the sheep are His rod and staff. The staff was often bent or hooked at one end, and a shepherd would use it to rescue a sheep by pulling it out of rocky crags or bushes it would get stuck in. Often times, we stray from the Lord and find ourselves stuck in sin or situations we don't want to be in. The Lord is good to come to our rescue by drawing us out of the pit and putting our feet on solid ground.

A shepherd would use the rod to prod his sheep down the road. The rod was also used to discipline the sheep that had strayed, to keep them close to the shepherd. It is noteworthy that the psalmist said that the rod comforted him. This teaches us that sometimes it is necessary for the Lord to discipline us when we stray from Him. This discipline is a comfort because it corrects us and points us down the path of righteousness.

Pause and Reflect

1 How does this picture of God being your Shepherd affect your view of Him?

---

2 What are some specific ways you have seen God use His rod and staff to comfort you? Take time to thank Him for this.

Imitators of Christ

1 Corinthians 10:32–11:1: "Give no offense to the Jews or the Greeks or the church of God, just as I also try to please all people in all things, not seeking my own profit, but the profit of many, so that they may be saved. Imitate me, as I also imitate Christ."

When we follow the voice of our Shepherd, Jesus, we should begin to mimic Him and reflect Him to others. Paul called the Corinthians to imitate him as he imitated Christ. Our walk should so closely mirror that of Christ's that if anyone followed us, they would essentially be following Jesus.

I once was driving on a highway when I saw a van drive past with an advertisement on the back of it that read, "Follow me to Dave's Pizza!" I remember thinking to myself that this van must always be heading toward Dave's Pizza. Suppose someone were to take the advice of this advertisement literally and begin following the van. If the driver were to stop at any other location, then he would have led the follower astray.

As Christians, we should pay careful attention to our manner of living. This is especially true because of our public witness as followers of Christ. Christians should embody the truth of Christ that they proclaim. Our lives should not lead people astray by giving them any reason not to follow Christ. If people were to follow us, would they end up at Jesus?

Pause and Reflect

1 Are there any areas of your life where you do not embody the truth you believe and profess?

2 What changes need to be made for you to mimic Christ in your daily life?

SHEEP OF OTHER FOLDS

John 10:16: "But I have other sheep that are not of this fold; I must bring them also, and they will listen to My voice. Then there will be one flock, one shepherd."

Jesus challenged His followers to remember that His mission is to draw sheep from other folds to Himself. This showed His followers that the good news of Jesus was not just for their clan but also for people of all tribes and races. The mission of God is to call one flock from all different peoples of the world to Himself as their Shepherd. To follow Jesus means that we are to move beyond our own people.

In Ephesians 2, Paul urges us to remember that all of us were at one time not part of God's people. Only through the blood of Christ have we become His own. Ephesians goes on to describe the church as the manifold wisdom of God. The word *manifold* means *multifaceted* or *to have multiple faces,* much like a sparkling diamond. When the church reflects people united in Christ from all over the world, it shines to the glory of God.

As His sheep, we must not fix our eyes merely inward but also out toward the lost sheep of other folds. We must leave our comfort zones and take the love of Christ to people who do not look or talk or dress like us. As we listen to the voice of Jesus and follow Him, our lives will embody His mission. To follow Christ is to care for and go after the sheep of other folds.

Pause and Reflect

1   In what ways can you begin to fix your eyes on others in pursuing the mission of Christ?

- -

2   Who are some people God is calling you to take the love of Christ to, even if you must leave your comfort zone?

Discussion Questions

1   In what ways does your view of pastors change when you recognize them as God's shepherds under the authority of Jesus, the Good Shepherd? What responsibilities does a shepherd have? How can a church affirm the shepherding gifts of those God sets apart for pastoral ministry?

2   What "little sheep" has God entrusted to your care (a small group, a young believer to disciple, your children)?

3   What can we learn from the example of humility set forth by Jesus in His washing of the disciples' feet? How could you model this type of servant leadership today?

4   Describe a time when you were impacted by a pastor who proclaimed the truth and lived it out. Is there someone in your life for whom you are modeling what it looks like to live out the teachings of Jesus?

5   What potential effect can pastors who do not practice what they preach have on their flock? Is your life more like Noah in that your faith influences others, or is it more like Lot in that your behavior is inconsistent with your beliefs?

6   Would you feel comfortable saying to someone, "Watch me, and follow me as I follow Christ"? Why or why not? What would need to change for you to be confident in showing others what it looks like to follow Jesus?

7   In what ways can pastors today put their own interests aside for the interests of the church? Can you think of an example when it was costly for a pastor to preach the truth? How can we encourage our pastors to fearlessly proclaim the truth despite opposition?

8   Can you give an example of an area in which it might be easier for a church to follow a trend of culture rather than stand firm for the truth of God?

9   In what ways does your life reflect or deny your eternal hope? How are your priorities affected when you think of the mission of God? What are some things God is calling you to leave behind in order to engage with Him in His mission to reach lost sheep?

10   How does Christ's return influence our evangelistic efforts?

Chapter 12

Perseverance

The King Preserves His People

VOICES FROM *the Church*

"For me, suffering is still that jackhammer breaking apart my rocks of resistance every day. It's still the chisel that God is using to chip away at my self-sufficiency and my self-motivation and my self-consumption. Suffering is still that sheepdog snapping and barking at my heels, driving me down the road to Calvary where otherwise I do not want to go…It is at Calvary, at the cross, where I meet suffering on God's terms."[1]

–Joni Eareckson Tada

VOICES FROM *Church History*

"It is wonderful to hold God's hand. But it is far more wonderful for God to hold our hand. And that's what God does when He saves us."[2]

–W. A. Criswell (1909-2002)

In the 1988 World Series, the Los Angeles Dodgers limped into the championship games without their best player—Kirk Gibson, who had been injured earlier in the season. To make matters worse, the Dodgers were facing the Oakland A's, the team with the best record. The prognosticators predicted an easy victory for the A's. But surprisingly, the first game ended with one of baseball's most memorable moments.

Going into the ninth inning, the Dodgers were behind by a run. The A's brought in their closer, who was practically unhittable. Some Dodgers fans left the game early, saddened at the expected outcome. With two outs in the bottom of the ninth, the Dodgers manager sent an injured Kirk Gibson to the plate. At his best, he would have a difficult time making it to first base fast enough. But to the shock of all in the stadium, Gibson hit the ball over the right field wall for the game-winning home run.

Interestingly enough, when you watch the replay, you can see the brake lights from a car in the parking lot as the driver slammed on the brakes, perhaps hearing the news on the radio. The fans who left missed a great moment in World Series history because they left early. They gave up hope when they thought the odds were stacked against them.

Today, many people are unaware that the Christian life will be marked with trials and struggles that test our faith. Too often people who claim to follow Christ head for the "parking lot" at the first sign of hardship and strife. They miss what God wants to accomplish through the trial.

The apostles Peter and John wrote letters to Christians who were battling persecution from outside the church and heresy from inside the church. These letters prepared Christians by informing them of the inevitability, purpose, and hope of trials. We can take heart in knowing that despite our earthly trials, temptations, and ongoing struggles with sin, Christ has promised to perfect the work He has begun in us.

God is glorified in the perseverance of His people through times of trial (1 Pet. 1:3-9).

3 *Praise the God and Father of our Lord Jesus Christ. According to His great mercy, He has given us a new birth into a living hope through the resurrection of Jesus Christ from the dead* 4 *and into an inheritance that is imperishable, uncorrupted, and unfading, kept in heaven for you.* 5 *You are being protected by God's power through faith for a salvation that is ready to be revealed in the last time.* 6 *You rejoice in this, though now for a short time you have had to struggle in various trials* 7 *so that the genuineness of your faith—more valuable than gold, which perishes though refined by fire—*

may result in praise, glory, and honor at the revelation of Jesus Christ. 8 *You love Him, though you have not seen Him. And though not seeing Him now, you believe in Him and rejoice with inexpressible and glorious joy,* 9 *because you are receiving the goal of your faith, the salvation of your souls.*

Peter's purpose in writing this passage was to give us hope. As soon as we are saved, we are birthed into a living hope (v. 3). We are saved (justified in the present) and are in the process of being sanctified (made holy). Throughout our lives, we become more like Christ until the day when Christ appears and we shall be like Him (glorified). This hope that we will be glorified—made perfect—is the inheritance (v. 4) and the goal of our faith (v. 9). If this is the goal, then how does God make us more like Christ during our lives?

Peter encouraged his readers by telling them that trials are one of God's primary means of refining us toward the goal of Christ-likeness (vv. 6-7). That's why we can rejoice. Trials are part of God's plan for us. When we follow Jesus Christ, the One who suffered for us, we can expect to suffer too. That's why, all around the world, Christians who endure suffering for the sake of the kingdom rejoice. They know their suffering confirms the truth that they belong to King Jesus and are progressing toward the goal of their faith.

It's worth remembering that just because a Christian may be going through suffering doesn't mean that he or she is experiencing Christian suffering (see 4:14). The kind of suffering Peter says is godly and purifying is the kind that comes as a result of following Jesus. While we should welcome this kind of suffering with joy, we should grieve the suffering that comes as a result of our sin. If we are insulted because of our faith, we should rejoice. But if we are insulted because we have wronged someone, we should repent.

Christians rejoice in trials by understanding their purpose. Peter wrote that suffering tests the genuineness of our faith just as gold is refined by fire (v. 7). If our greatest desire is to become more like Jesus, then we will find joy in anything that purifies us and makes us more like Him.

Peter claimed that the testing of believers ultimately results in the glory of God (v. 7). God receives glory from our faith being tested. Why? Because we are given the opportunity to express our trust in the greater purpose God has for the trial we are facing.

We see this principle played out in God's call of Abraham to offer up his son Isaac as a sacrifice. The first verse of Genesis 22 tells us that God "tested" Abraham when He called him. This call seemed to go against the promise of God that his offspring would be called through Isaac. In the Book of Hebrews, we learn that Abraham trusted that God could even raise Isaac from the dead if necessary (Heb. 11:19). Abraham's genuine faith was revealed because he trusted that somehow God was going to keep His promise, and through that testing, God received the glory when God Himself provided the sacrifice to take the place of Isaac.

It's no wonder that Christians would be known for faithful suffering. After all, Jesus—the Messiah we follow—trusted God's plan when He willingly laid down His life. What better example of genuine faith resulting in the glory of God than Jesus' resurrection from the dead! And Christ's resurrection forms the basis for the living hope that we have today (v. 3). Jesus declared, "You will have suffering in this world. Be courageous! I have conquered the world" (John 16:33).

Believers today stand firm in the trials they can see by believing and trusting in the Jesus they can't (1 Pet. 1:8). The apostle Peter also wrote that those who suffer according to God's will should entrust their souls to the faithful Creator while continuing to do good (4:19). By trusting our Savior and continuing to follow Him in the midst of a trial, we bring God glory because we put on display our faith that He is faithful even in bad times.

A few years ago, I went through a two-week period when I suffered from panic and anxiety attacks. The only way I made it through that dark time was by clinging to Jesus and trusting that He was faithful to His promises even in trying times.

A couple years later, my non-Christian brother called me after going through a similar bout of anxiety. I told him that until he turned his life over to Jesus, he would never have complete peace in his soul. I shared several verses of Scripture with him, verses that had helped me through my own anxiety. During that time, my brother saw he needed Jesus. We prayed together as he repented and trusted in Christ. Today I look back on a dark moment in my life and am thankful that God used it for His glorious purposes and to rescue my brother from sin.

God's people persevere in light of the promised new heavens and new earth (2 Pet. 3:8-13).

8 *Dear friends, don't let this one thing escape you: With the Lord one day is like a thousand years, and a thousand years like one day.* 9 *The Lord does not delay His promise, as some understand delay, but is patient with you, not wanting any to perish but all to come to repentance.*

10 *But the Day of the Lord will come like a thief; on that day the heavens will pass away with a loud noise, the elements will burn and be dissolved, and the earth and the works on it will be disclosed.* 11 *Since all these things are to be destroyed in this way, it is clear what sort of people you should be in holy conduct and godliness* 12 *as you wait for and earnestly desire the coming of the day of God. The heavens will be on fire and be dissolved because of it, and the elements will melt with the heat.* 13 *But based on His promise, we wait for the new heavens and a new earth, where righteousness will dwell.*

Being raised in an Iranian family, my first language was Farsi. I learned English from a tutor who read to me every day after school. In the second grade, she gave me a small New Testament. Ten years later, I read that New Testament and came to faith in Christ.

Since my father was a prominent Muslim, I stayed quiet about my newfound faith. After a year and a half of hiding my Bible and sneaking away to church, my father finally found out. He made me choose between being his son and following Christ. By God's strength, I chose Jesus. My father disowned me.

That night, I reread the Scriptures where Jesus taught us to love Him over our father and mother (Matt. 10:37-39). Having experienced this rejection from my father, I had a hard time showing him love. But as the Lord impressed on me the reality of His patient, unfailing love for me, I was compelled to have patience and love for my father.

How are we to respond when we face trials because of our faith? Peter pointed to God's patient character. As we remember how Christ showed us patience and how God's heart is for all to respond to Him in repentance and faith, we are filled with the same compassion. We persevere in patience toward those who oppose us.

Peter also reminded his readers of the coming Day of the Lord, when God will keep His promises and flood the world with His justice (2 Pet. 3:10-12). This helps us persevere when we see injustice in this world because we know it is temporary. The psalmist wrote, "Be silent before the LORD and wait expectantly for Him; do not be agitated by one who prospers in his way, by the man who carries out evil plans" (Ps. 37:7).

The story of Job is another example of patience in the midst of injustice. Job had suffered much personal loss. His closest friends were wrong to attribute this loss to his sin. Job held fast to his integrity before the Lord and declared his faith that he would be vindicated in the end (Job 13:18). He maintained his faith in God's promise of justice.

God's coming justice and His punishment of the ungodly should cause us to move with compassion toward those who presume on His patience. Every breath we take is given to us by a gracious God. He is patient toward those who persist in rejecting His good news. We too must be patient, even as we plead with people to repent and trust Jesus.

When our eyes are set on this fallen world, our hearts fail and our knees buckle under the weight of suffering and pain. But when we fix our eyes on the coming kingdom where righteousness dwells (2 Pet. 3:13), we can withstand the trials of this world: the trials that come against us from outside (persecution) and the trials from within (our ongoing struggle with sin).

Because we know the final outcome of this world, we can withstand our temporary trials. Without this knowledge, we would be left with despair and anxiety at almost every turn.

I remember a time I was going to miss watching a football game. I set up the game to be recorded so I could watch it later. That evening, I received bad updates from others. My team was getting beat. But by the end, my team came back and won. When I watched the game later, my reactions were different. When my team was behind by 21 points, I was still smiling. I knew the outcome. Instead of ranting when a player fumbled the ball, I pumped my fist with excitement because I knew they were going to come back and win.

Of course, real life adversity does not yield smiles and fist pumps. Even so, because Christians know the "final score," we can maintain a sense of joy that overcomes us in the midst of our struggle. We anticipate seeing how God will put even bad events into service for our ultimate good and His glory.

God's people demonstrate their perseverance by their actions (1 John 2:15-19).

15 *Do not love the world or the things that belong to the world. If anyone loves the world, love for the Father is not in him.* 16 *For everything that belongs to the world—the lust of the flesh, the lust of the eyes, and the pride in one's lifestyle—is not from the Father, but is from the world.* 17 *And the world with its lust is passing away, but the one who does God's will remains forever.*

18 *Children, it is the last hour. And as you have heard, "Antichrist is coming," even now many antichrists have come. We know from this that it is the last hour.* 19 *They went out from us, but they did not belong to us; for if they had belonged to us, they would have remained with us. However, they went out so that it might be made clear that none of them belongs to us.*

Earlier we saw how Peter encouraged Christians who faced persecution from those outside the church. Here we see how John warned against "false Christians," or "antichrists," who show by their disobedience that they do not belong to Christ.

In this letter, the apostle John showed that genuine Christians do not run back to the world from which they were called. Christians love God, not the world, and this love is manifested in their persevering faith. Persevering in obedience does not mean Christians have to maintain their salvation. Neither does it mean Christians no longer sin. This doctrine speaks to the truth that those who belong to Christ will demonstrate their faith by their obedience.

John taught that perseverance is not just a passive enduring of trials but an active fulfilling of the will of God. He reminded his readers that all of the pursuits and desires of the world will pass away. But genuine Christians pursue the will of God and demonstrate their faith through their obedience (v. 17). We are not called just to say no to the world but to say yes to God.

Whenever we talk about good works, it's important to remember that our good works do not save us or keep us saved. Instead, they are the evidence of true faith. Many object to the free gift of salvation because they worry that grace removes the burden of doing good works. They think that if the threat of eternal punishment is taken away, no one will have any reason to live for God.

But Scripture is clear that grace does not squelch a Christian's good works. Instead, it fuels them. Because of God's grace, we are now free to live righteously. We've been set free from sin and no longer want to displease God. Good works are not a means to our salvation but rather a product or proof of our salvation.

Two years after my father disowned me for being a Christian, he welcomed me back into his good graces so long as I would fulfill his dream for me, which was to become a medical doctor. I knew in my heart that God was calling me to full-time ministry, but I ran from God's call because I didn't want to disappoint my father a second time. My sister, who also became a Christian, wrote me a letter in which she confronted me of running from God's will, and she quoted 1 John 2:17: "the one who does God's will remains forever."

One of the hardest things I have ever had to do in my life was to take my father to lunch and break the news to him that I was not going to medical school but instead going to seminary to train for pastoral ministry. This led to another breaking of my relationship with my father. However, the words of Matthew 16:25 are true—as I have lost my life, I have found life in Christ. All these years later, I would never trade the countless opportunities the Lord has given me to minister the Gospel both in America and overseas for what my life could have been. Today, I could be a doctor and my father would be proud of me. Additionally, I could've avoided one of the greatest trials of my life. But I would've missed seeing what God was going to do through my trial for His glory!

Conclusion

The Christian will face trials and tribulations. But we can rest assured that the Lord who called us will also preserve us. By persevering in obedience, we demonstrate the genuineness of our faith.

Christians can rejoice in the midst of trials because we belong to the King who promises to preserve His people. Christians persevere by remembering that God has a greater purpose in trials. Suffering is often the tool of God to chisel us into the image of Christ. Our faith is strengthened when we keep our eyes on the hope of glory, the day when earthly trials give way to eternal righteousness in the presence of the King.

- -

PRAYER OF *Response*

There is mercy with You, O Lord, and exceeding riches in Your kindness through Jesus. May I always feel my need of Him. Let Your restored joy be my strength. May it keep me from lusting after the world, bear up heart and mind in loss of comforts, enliven me in the valley of death, work in me the image of the heavenly, and give me to enjoy the first fruits of spirituality. [3]

–Puritan prayer, adapted

Devotions

Suffering as Ministry

2 Corinthians 1:3-4: "Praise the God and Father of our Lord Jesus Christ, the Father of mercies and the God of all comfort. He comforts us in all our affliction, so that we may be able to comfort those who are in any kind of affliction, through the comfort we ourselves receive from God."

When we experience suffering and trials, there is a tendency to be inward-focused. We are consumed with thoughts of how the present difficulty is affecting us. Of course, this is a natural tendency. But at the beginning of his second letter to the Corinthians, Paul encouraged Christians to focus outward in suffering. Whenever our focus shifts outward, the weight of our troubles seems to lessen.

It is interesting how the word "comfort" in this passage alternates between being a verb and a noun. Comfort is something God does (verb) and also something we receive (noun). Comfort is something we do (verb) and others receive (noun). God is described as the God of all comfort who comforts us. But then Paul used a key phrase when he said that God does this "so that" we can comfort others with the comfort we have received. In other words, God has purpose for comforting us. God desires our comfort to become a ministry to others.

As a body, Christians are called to share abundantly in suffering and comfort. When others go through suffering, we are called to walk beside them and help them carry the burden of their trial. One of the ways we do this is by sharing the comfort we have received from God in our own suffering. When this happens, God is actually the One who is comforting through us.

Pause and Reflect

1   In what areas of your life do you tend to be inward-focused on your troubles?

----

2   How can you use the comfort you have received to minister to others today?

Purposeful Suffering

Romans 5:3-5: "And not only that, but we also rejoice in our afflictions, because we know that affliction produces endurance, endurance produces proven character, and proven character produces hope. This hope will not disappoint us, because God's love has been poured out in our hearts through the Holy Spirit who was given to us."

Many truths in the Christian faith go against the grain of conventional thinking. Joy in suffering is one such truth. People may wonder how it is possible for there to be any good in suffering. Why should anyone rejoice in it?

In Romans, Paul wrote that Christians should rejoice in suffering because we know we belong to a God who has a purpose for all things, including our hardships. He said that suffering prepares us for future trials by producing endurance in us. This endurance, in turn, produces character in us. In Philippians 3, Paul wrote about sharing in Christ's sufferings and becoming like Him in His death. God uses trials in our life to instill Christlike character in us.

For this reason, Paul could say that the end result of suffering is hope because it is what makes us more like Christ. 1 John 3 reminds us that at the end of life, we know that we will be like Christ. This truth gives us hope.

If your goal in life is reduced to whatever this world can give you, then there is no hope in suffering. But if your goal in life is to become like Christ, there is incredible hope in suffering. Since God has poured His love into us and given us the Holy Spirit, we know that as our loving Father, He will accomplish His purpose in our trials.

Pause and Reflect

1   How does your goal for life impact the way you view suffering?

- -

2   What are some ways God has used trials to produce good fruit in your life?

Suffering on Mission

2 Timothy 2:8-10: "Keep your attention on Jesus Christ as risen from the dead and descended from David. This is according to my gospel. I suffer for it to the point of being bound like a criminal, but God's message is not bound. This is why I endure all things for the elect: so that they also may obtain salvation, which is in Christ Jesus, with eternal glory."

In this passage, Paul revealed to Timothy what his motivation was in enduring persecution. He was suffering for the sake of the gospel and for those who would come to faith in Christ. Paul understood that this world was temporary, and he was concerned with living his life to impact the spiritual life of others (2 Cor. 5:16).

With an eternal perspective, a Christian sees suffering as an opportunity rather than a setback. Paul told Timothy that though he was bound in chains, the Word of God was free to advance. Paul told the Philippians that he was imprisoned for Christ and that his chains were actually serving to advance the gospel (Phil. 1:12).

Today, there are many areas where Christians are being imprisoned for sharing the gospel. One might think this would hinder God's work. On the contrary, the gospel is thriving even in places where persecution of the Christian faith is increasing.

In our society, we may not go through the same kind of persecution as Christians in hostile environments. This does not mean there is not opposition to be faced in living on mission in the West. We may be shunned by peers, ridiculed, or disregarded by many for proclaiming Jesus. We may have to suffer the loss of jobs, promotions, friends, etc. As we endure these kinds of trials, we can press on in the hope that God may use us to eternally impact the world with the gospel.

Pause and Reflect

1   Do you encounter any opposition in your life for following Jesus? Why or why not?

- -

2   What are some ways that God has used "chains" in your life to advance the gospel?

Discussion Questions

1 Why was the surprise and glory of Gibson's World Series home run enhanced by his injury and the seemingly unbeatable odds against the team? Why are we often inspired by stories of underdogs? In what ways do trials and hardship increase our joy when we are victorious?

----

2 When was the last time you suffered as a result of your faith? How did you respond to that trial? What was your perspective of the trial at the time? How has your perspective changed? How did God use that trial to glorify Himself and mold you into the image of Christ?

----

3 How can Paul confidently state in Romans 8:28 that God is working all things together for the believer's good? What kind of perspective supports this statement? How does reorienting our suffering around Christ's glory help us through trials?

----

4 How does our understanding that people live forever—either in heaven or hell—influence the way we look at those around us? How does this truth lead us to mission?

----

5 In what ways does our future hope give us present hope in times of trial? What are some practical ways we can focus on eternity in order to persevere today? What are some examples in Scripture of men and women persevering in trials because they knew the "final score"?

----

6 How does our joyfulness in times of suffering display before the world the truth that Christ is to be treasured above all things?

----

7 Have you ever known someone who looked the part of a Christian but whose actions revealed that they did not know God? How should 1 John 2:19 inform the way we relate to other believers?

----

8 In your life, what are some ways that saying yes to the will of God will result in inward struggle or persecution from the world? How is perseverance demonstrated in our witness?

----

9 How can a Christian persevere against the lust of the flesh, the lust of the eyes, and the pride in one's lifestyle?

Chapter 13

The Consummation

The King Returns to Live with His People

The movie *Braveheart* has a scene when the Scottish army stands on the battlefield outnumbered by the English three to one. In light of the circumstances, some of the warriors begin to walk away. They assume their fight for independence is a lost cause.

Then the hero, William Wallace, shows up. When asked why they are leaving, the men say they would rather retreat and live than fight and die. Wallace acknowledges that running would ensure a longer life. Yet he calls them to imagine lying on their deathbeds in the future. Would they be willing to trade in those few extra days in order to make a stand for freedom? The speech stirs the Scots to unite and fight. They defeat the English despite the odds.

Wallace succeeded in convincing his compatriots to carry on the fight by leading them to take their eyes off of the temporary and to fix them on something more important that would transcend their lifespan—freedom for Scotland. When their perspective changed, their attitudes changed too. There was a transformation in the way they conducted themselves.

In the same way, the New Testament calls believers to shift focus from this temporary world to the returning King Jesus and His kingdom. This eternal perspective informs the way Christians live in this present world.

In this chapter, we will look at what the Bible has to say about the future of our world. As Christians, we look forward to the day when Christ will return to judge the living and the dead and finally purge this world of all traces of evil and unrighteousness. The reality of heaven and hell and the truth of Christ's second coming should impact the way we live. God calls us to look forward to Christ's coming with eager anticipation as we engage in His mission until He returns.

The truth of Christ's coming in the future should change our lives today (1 Thess. 1:8-10).

8 *For the Lord's message rang out from you, not only in Macedonia and Achaia, but in every place that your faith in God has gone out. Therefore, we don't need to say anything,* 9 *for they themselves report what kind of reception we had from you: how you turned to God from idols to serve the living and true God* 10 *and to wait for His Son from heaven, whom He raised from the dead—Jesus, who rescues us from the coming wrath.*

The apostle Paul encouraged the church in Thessalonica by mentioning how others were reporting on the signs of their Christian faith. These believers had turned from idols to serve God, certainly the mark of someone who has been transformed by the gospel.

Because of Christ, we gain an eternal perspective on the world. As the Spirit works in us, we begin to long for God more than earthly things. Longing for Christ is one of the marks of someone the gospel has transformed. We turn away from idols because we know they are a sham. We know only God can fulfill us. When Christ alters our perspective, we realize that the world and its desires are passing away (1 John 2:17). That's why the Christian longs for the true, living, and eternal God.

Notice how Paul pointed out the Thessalonians' eager longing for Christ's return as evidence of their faith. Turning away from the idols in our past goes along with turning toward the salvation promised in our future.

This waiting is not passive but active. Think of a waiter who waits on a table. A good waiter is always alert and attentive. In the same way, Christians must not give in to slumber or passivity. We go about serving others as we actively anticipate the return of Christ.

But how can we wait on Christ when we don't know the time of His return? Some Christians throw their hands up and suppose that uncertainty of the time means no need to be prepared. They're like a writer with no looming deadline and therefore no sense of urgency. But Jesus urged His disciples to act differently. The fact that we don't know the day He is coming is precisely the reason why we should stay alert (Matt. 24:42).

Other Christians get so fixated on trying to figure out when and how Christ will return that they neglect to prepare. They're like a single man or woman so consumed with finding the right person to marry that they fail to prepare themselves to *be* the right person to marry. Our ignorance of the day and hour of Christ's return should not spur us into a vain pursuit of dates and signs. Rather, we ought to assume Jesus will come suddenly and focus on being prepared.

Later in this letter, Paul claimed that the Day of the Lord would come like a thief in the night (1 Thess 5:2). Therefore, Christians ought not to sleep as others do but stay awake and sober (v. 6). The Thessalonians were to remain awake and sober as they waited on Christ.

Paul also reminded the Thessalonians that the One who is their hope, Jesus, is also the Savior who rescues them from the coming wrath. The knowledge of the wrath to come should remind us that God's justice will win out in the end. God will judge the evil of this world when Christ comes again. Knowing that judgment is on the horizon should create in us a sense of urgency in evangelism as we are filled with compassion toward those who do not know King Jesus.

The truth of Christ's coming leads us to reject the spirit of antichrist (2 Thess. 2:1-4).

In his next letter to the same church, Paul reassured believers that the Day of the Lord had not yet arrived. Apparently the church had heard false rumors of the Lord's coming and were doubting the legitimacy of His returning to gather them.

1 *Now concerning the coming of our Lord Jesus Christ and our being gathered to Him: We ask you, brothers,* 2 *not to be easily upset in mind or troubled, either by a spirit or by a message or by a letter as if from us, alleging that the Day of the Lord has come.* 3 *Don't let anyone deceive you in any way. For that day will not come unless the apostasy comes first and the man of lawlessness is revealed, the son of destruction.* 4 *He opposes and exalts himself above every so-called god or object of worship, so that he sits in God's sanctuary, publicizing that he himself is God.*

There is considerable debate over the identity of the "man of lawlessness." Many believe this is a reference to the beast, or the antichrist, portrayed in Revelation. Regardless of your view of this man's identity, it is clear that Paul urged the Christians in Thessalonica to reject the spirit of antichrist and stand firm in their faith lest they be swept up in the course of this world.

This man of lawlessness is characterized by self-exaltation. He opposes God's glory. He is not Satan, but he comes by the working of Satan (2 Thess. 2:9). He sets himself against God.

As fallen sinners, human beings are constantly seeking our own glory, even though we were originally made for God's glory and thus will never be fulfilled by seeking our own. The good news is that Jesus has redeemed us from this curse so we may now live for God's glory (2 Cor. 5:14-15). That's why it makes no sense for Christians to follow the way of the world when we know Jesus is coming to ultimately thwart the antichrist and put an end to human rebellion once and for all so that He might reign forever.

Paul also warned the Thessalonians to reject the spirit of rebellion that will prevail before the revealing of the mysterious man of lawlessness. Many interpreters believe Paul saw the world as becoming increasingly opposed and hostile to truth. That's why he urged people not to let anyone deceive them.

Like the Bereans in Acts 17:11, believers must run every claim through the filter of Scripture. The apostle John called his readers to test every spirit to see whether it belonged to God or antichrist. God's Word has been given to keep us afloat in the sea of this world (John 17:14). Abiding in Scripture is the anchor for a believer's soul in a culture swept up in the wave of lies.

The man of lawlessness is also defined by his opposition to holiness. He is therefore labeled "the son of destruction." In Ephesians 2, we learn that all of us were at one point following the course of the world, enslaved to fulfill our fleshly desires and marked for the coming wrath. But Christians have been made alive in Christ and therefore have the power of the Holy Spirit to be able to resist joining in the world's decadence.

In 1 Peter 4:4, we are told that the world is "surprised that you don't plunge with them into the same flood of wild living." Christians are to be like salmon swimming against the stream of this world. Lawlessness leads people to believe that they are not held accountable and can therefore do whatever pleases them. But Peter urged his readers to remain self-controlled because the end of all things is at hand (v. 7). The truth of Christ's coming leads us to reject the spirit of lawlessness and pursue holiness.

The truth of Christ's coming gives us urgency in joining God's mission (Jude 20-23).

The late Steve Jobs said this at a commencement speech: "Remembering that I'll be dead soon is the most important tool I've ever encountered to help me make the big choices in life…[All external expectations, all pride, all fear of embarrassment or failure] just fall away in the face of death, leaving only what is truly important." The reality of death makes people evaluate what is truly important in life. But especially in the case of Christians, our hope of eternal life should cause us to reevaluate our temporal life.

20 *But you, dear friends, as you build yourselves up in your most holy faith and pray in the Holy Spirit,* 21 *keep yourselves in the love of God, expecting the mercy of our Lord Jesus Christ for eternal life.* 22 *Have mercy on those who doubt;* 23 *save others by snatching them from the fire; have mercy on others but with fear, hating even the garment defiled by the flesh.*

This passage helps Christians focus on what is truly important. Along with the reality of death, the truth of Christ's coming should give us urgency to engage the world on mission for Christ. In light of eternity, our lifetime is limited. We must ask what the Lord's purpose is for our days on this earth.

In John 17, Jesus prayed for His disciples. He said that the world does not love them because they are not of the world (v. 14). If we, as disciples of Christ, know that we don't belong to the world, then why does Jesus leave us in the world? He declared that He was sending the disciples into the world for those who will believe through their word (vv. 18,20).

Knowledge of the coming judgment on those who don't know Jesus should be a strong motivator to be on mission for Christ. Jude stressed the urgency by calling us to snatch them out of the fire. Remembering that all of us were under condemnation and headed for the wrath of God before Christ rescued us should humble us and drive us to point others to the Deliverer.

Paul understood this truth well. He wrote, "Therefore, because we know the fear of the Lord, we seek to persuade people" (2 Cor. 5:11). The salvation he received did not move him to complacency but to action. In Athens, he saw that the city was given over to idols, and his spirit was provoked within him. So he went into the synagogue to persuade the Jews and into the marketplace to convince the Greeks of their need for Christ (Acts 17:16-17).

Just as Jesus left His place in glory to come into a broken world to save us, we must get out of our comfort zones, go into the world, and meet people where they are. The gospel doesn't call us just to congregate in church buildings but to enter the world with the message of hope in Christ.

The result of Christ's coming is a renewed earth filled with God's presence (Rev. 21:1-8).

1 *Then I saw a new heaven and a new earth, for the first heaven and the first earth had passed away, and the sea no longer existed.* 2 *I also saw the Holy City, new Jerusalem, coming down out of heaven from God, prepared like a bride adorned for her husband.*

3 *Then I heard a loud voice from the throne:*
Look! God's dwelling is with humanity, and He will live with them.
They will be His people,
and God Himself will be with them and be their God.
4 *He will wipe away every tear from their eyes.*
Death will no longer exist; grief, crying, and pain will exist no longer,
because the previous things have passed away.
5 *Then the One seated on the throne said, "Look! I am making everything new." He also said, "Write, because these words are faithful and true."* 6 *And He said to me, "It is done! I am the Alpha and the Omega, the Beginning and the End. I will give water as a gift to the thirsty from the spring of life.* 7 *The victor will inherit these things, and I will be his God, and he will be My son.* 8 *But the cowards, unbelievers, vile, murderers, sexually immoral, sorcerers, idolaters, and all liars—their share will be in the lake that burns with fire and sulfur, which is the second death."*

In this vision given to the apostle John, God has promised to make all things new. After the destruction of Satan, God will renew the created order of heaven and earth to be a dwelling place for Himself and His bride, the church. This echoes a prophecy given to Isaiah: God will create a new heaven and a new earth, and the former things shall not be remembered (Isa. 65:17).

Let's consider the characteristics of this new cosmos. We see here the vision of a new city coming down from heaven from God. He is the One who has prepared and created this new city for Himself and His people.

The Book of Hebrews tells us that Abraham looked forward to a heavenly city whose builder and designer was God (Heb. 11:10). God told Abraham that He would make a people for Himself out of Abraham and that He would give them a land. The promised land that God swore to Abraham was a precursor to the better and heavenly one—a city that God has prepared for His people (v. 16). We have the hope that with the return of Christ, we will dwell as citizens in a "new Jerusalem."

In this vision, we also receive the wonderful promise of God's renewed presence with us for eternity. From start to finish, the Bible is the story of God's redemption of the world. When Adam and Eve sinned in Genesis 3, they were removed from the garden of Eden, out from the presence of God. But God made a promise to Abraham and his offspring: "I will be their God and they shall be My people." That promise is woven into the whole story of redemption. It is the promise God gave to Israel when He redeemed them from slavery and made them into a nation (Ex. 6:7; Lev. 26:12). After they were exiled from the promised land because of their sin, God promised to restore Israel by pointing to this same promise (Jer. 31:33; Ezek. 11:20).

In Jesus' life, God came to dwell with man in a far more intimate way, by taking on human flesh (Matt. 1:23; cf. Isa. 7:14). As a result of Christ's work, God now dwells within every believer through His Holy Spirit (2 Cor. 6:16-18). And at the end of time, God will destroy all sin, renew the earth, raise up our bodies, and dwell with us fully and permanently in a renewed Eden. Hence, the Bible ends with the renewal of this promise: "Look! God's dwelling is with humanity, and He will live with them. They will be His people, and God Himself will be with them and be their God" (Rev. 21:3).

To be in the presence of God for eternity is our greatest promise and hope. David's one desire was to dwell in the house of the Lord forever (Ps. 27:4). We see in David what man was originally created for—to know God intimately. Jesus said in John 17:3, "This is eternal life: that they may know You, the only true God, and the One You have sent—Jesus Christ."

The purpose for Christ's first coming was to make a way for us to be in God's presence. The purpose for His second coming is that we will be present with Him for eternity. If Jesus Himself is the greatest treasure in heaven, then He must be our greatest treasure on earth.

Finally, we see that the new cosmic order will be markedly different than the old one. The old creation was infected by evil and sin, in bondage to corruption (Rom. 8:21). This first creation will melt away and give way to a new heavens and earth in which righteousness dwells (2 Pet. 3:12-13).

For those who belong to Christ, this eternal home will be a place where death and grief no longer exist. The curse of death will be done away with forever because our perishable, mortal bodies will be renewed into imperishable, immortal bodies. Those who have put their faith in Christ in this world will be free to enjoy and cherish Him for eternity.

Conclusion

Too often we believe the old lie that this world will fulfill us. But the truth of Christ's coming should strengthen our hope in Jesus, who supersedes all worldly things. As Christians, we are on a journey to a coming kingdom where we will be free from this fallen world and dwell with God forever!

- -

VOICES FROM *the Church*

"Far from sitting on clouds playing harps, as people often imagine, the redeemed people of God in the new world will be the agents of his love going out in new ways, to accomplish new creative tasks, to celebrate and extend the glory of his love."[2]

–N. T. Wright

Devotions

THE PROMISED LAND

Hebrews 11:13-16: "These all died in faith without having received the promises, but they saw them from a distance, greeted them, and confessed that they were foreigners and temporary residents on the earth. Now those who say such things make it clear that they are seeking a homeland. If they were thinking about where they came from, they would have had an opportunity to return. But they now desire a better place—a heavenly one. Therefore God is not ashamed to be called their God, for He has prepared a city for them."

The great heroes of our faith listed in Hebrews 11 lived in the gap between the country they came out of and the land God had promised them. Abraham was called to leave his father's country and go to a land where God would make a great nation out of his descendants.

Just like Abraham and these Hebrews 11 saints, followers of Christ live in a gap as *strangers* and *exiles* on the earth. As Paul said, "our citizenship is in heaven, from which we also eagerly wait for a Savior, the Lord Jesus Christ" (Phil. 3:20). It is important that we acknowledge our situation and have the right perspective on our lives.

We learn from Hebrews 11 that these saints weren't even thinking about the land they came out of but were looking ahead to the better country that the Lord was preparing for them. We must not look back and long for our former life before Christ. We must acknowledge that we are passing through and that the present world does not offer any lasting fulfillment. So where do we place our hope? Our hope is in Jesus and for the day He returns to renew creation and dwell with us forever.

Pause and Reflect

1   How would your life change if it truly reflected the truth that you are a pilgrim in this world longing for a future home?

- -

2   In what ways could you spend your days here pursuing the things that will last in eternity?

A Faithful Servant

Matthew 24:45-46: "Who then is a faithful and sensible slave, whom his master has put in charge of his household, to give them food at the proper time? That slave whose master finds him working when he comes will be rewarded."

This parable is set in the heart of Jesus' teaching on the day of the Lord's coming. Jesus had just told his disciples that His second coming would be at an hour that is not expected.

The faithful and wise servant is described as the one who is fulfilling his master's task when he returns. The task is described as taking care of the master's house and providing food.

The parable goes on to contrast this faithful servant with the wicked servant. The wicked servant is the one who assumes his master is delayed and not only forgets his task but mistreats his fellow servants. This self-centered servant eats and drinks with drunkards only seeking to fill his own belly. Jesus said this servant will be in for a rude awakening when his master suddenly returns.

Christians are called to actively wait for Christ's return by striving to be faithful with the task the Lord has left for us. Our task is to serve others as we fulfill the Great Commission to make disciples of all nations. The degree to which we are anticipating Christ's return will be reflected in the degree to which we give our lives for others to advance the gospel. We must not be lulled into thinking His return is in the distant future and thus focus merely on taking care of ourselves. If we believe His return is imminent, then we will be found faithful in serving others.

Pause and Reflect

1   In what ways have you been lulled into forgetting Christ's return and thus forgetting your task?

---

2   How can you move into an active waiting on Christ as you fulfill your calling?

Enduring to the End on Mission

Matthew 24:11-14: "Many false prophets will rise up and deceive many. Because lawlessness will multiply, the love of many will grow cold. But the one who endures to the end will be delivered. This good news of the kingdom will be proclaimed in all the world as a testimony to all nations. And then the end will come."

Jesus told his disciples of the end times when many will fall away, hate one another, and grow cold in their love for God. He encouraged them not to be one of these and to endure to the end. Then the Lord commissioned them to proclaim the gospel to the entire world. Our love will remain strong for the Lord as we join Him in ushering in His kingdom by taking His truth to our world. We must focus our efforts on that which will last for eternity.

A friend of mine often talked of his mentor who led him to Christ and discipled him as a young Christian. When his mentor passed away, my friend went home for his funeral. When he returned, he recounted an incredible moment during the funeral. The pastor asked those in the audience who had been influenced to follow Christ through the life of this dear saint to stand to their feet. My friend was delighted to stand in honor of his mentor but was shocked to find he was not close to being the only one. He said he saw a sea of men rising to their feet. We must be a people who invest our lives in eternity by being on mission to proclaim Christ in every place our lives take us.

Pause and Reflect

1   Who would stand at your funeral because the Lord used you to influence them for Christ?

- -

2   How can you be more intentional to be on mission at home, work, etc.?

Discussion Questions

1   In what areas of your life do you need a shift in perspective from the temporary to the eternal? How does knowing the end of the Bible's story give us confidence and hope today?

---

2   Can you recall a time when a life-or-death event took place and immediately rearranged all your priorities?

---

3   In what ways does the Enemy tempt us to long for idols rather than God for fulfillment? What's the connection between turning from idols and waiting for Christ's return?

---

4   How would you live your life differently if you knew Jesus were returning this week? What would you pursue more? What would you set aside?

---

5   How does the knowledge of the wrath of God change the way you view earthly desires? How does the truth that God will be the One to execute justice change the way you view those who have wronged you?

---

6   What are some ways in which people in our culture actively oppose God? What are some common traits we would expect to see in someone who follows the way of this world?

---

7   What are some ways we can stay on guard against false teaching? Have you ever denied or shied away from God's truth because of cultural pressures? In what areas of your life are you following the course of this world and doing whatever pleases you?

---

8   Do you sense a burden for those who don't know Christ? Why or why not? What are some ways you can enter the world and proclaim the gospel in your daily life?

---

9   How have you traditionally viewed heaven? What are some popular misconceptions about heaven? How does the vision of a renewed earth affect our view of work, rest, and worship today? What do you see that was broken by sin now being reconciled and restored?

---

10   Do you long to be in God's presence in your daily life? Why or why not? What are some changes you can make in your daily life to ensure time with Jesus?

Endnotes

Chapter 1

1. J. I. Packer, *Knowing God* (Downers Grove: IVP Books, 1973), 53.

Chapter 2

1. C. S. Lewis, *The Quotable Lewis*, eds. Wayne Martindale and Jerry Root (Carol Stream, IL: Tyndale House Publishers, Inc., 1990), 340.
2. Daniel M. Doriani, *The Sermon on the Mount: The Character of a Disciple* (Phillipsburg, NJ: P&R Publishing, 2006), 223.
3. Ed Stetzer and Philip Nation, *Compelled* (Birmingham, AL: New Hope Publishers, 2012), 88.
4. Jonathan Leeman, *Reverberation* (Chicago: Moody Publishers, 2011), 19.
5. Cyril of Alexandria, "Homily 41," in *Commentary on the Gospel of St. Luke*, trans. R. Payne Smith (Long Island, NY: Studion Publishers, Inc., 1983), 178, quoted in *Luke*, ed. Arthur A. Just Jr., vol. III in *Ancient Christian Commentary on Scripture: New Testament* (Downers Grove: InterVarsity Press, 2003), 132.

Chapter 3

1. Paige Patterson, "The Work of Christ," in *A Theology for the Church*, ed. Daniel L. Akin (Nashville: B&H Academic, 2007), 548.
2. Cyril of Alexandria, *Commentary on the Gospel of John*, 3.4, quoted in *A Library of Fathers of the Holy Catholic Church Anterior to the Division of the East and West*, trans. members of the English Church, vol. 43 (Oxford: John Henry Parker, 1800-1881), 324-25, quoted in *John 1–10*, ed. Joel C. Elowsky, vol. IVa in *Ancient Christian Commentary on Scripture: New Testament* (Downers Grove: InterVarsity Press, 2006), 211.
3. C. S. Lewis, *The Weight of Glory* (New York: HarperOne, 1976), 31.

Chapter 4

1. Edward Shillito, "Jesus of the Scars," in *Jesus of the Scars and Other Poems* (London: Hodder & Stoughton, 1919), quoted in *The God Who Is There* (Grand Rapids: Baker Books, 2010), 162.
2. Dietrich Bonhoeffer, *The Cost of Discipleship* (New York: Simon & Schuster, 1959), 89, 91.
3. Charles Spurgeon, "Risen with Christ," GodRules.net [online], 28 March 1880 [cited 11 September 2012]. Available from the Internet: *www.godrules.net.*

Chapter 5

1. John R. W. Stott, *Christ the Controversialist* (Downers Grove: Inter-Varsity Press, 1970), 61.
2. G. K. Chesterton, *The Everlasting Man* (eBook: Lulu.com, 2007), 192.

Chapter 6

1. Michael Williams, *How to Read the Bible Through the Jesus Lens* (Grand Rapids: Zondervan, 2012), 178.
2. John Stott, *The Living Church* (Downers Grove: InterVarsity Press, 2007), 32.
3. William D. Mounce, gen. ed., "Church: New Testament," in *Mounce's Complete Expository Dictionary of Old & New Testament Words* (Grand Rapids: Zondervan, 2006), 110.

Chapter 7

1. Martin Luther, *Commentary on the Epistle to the Galatians* (eBook: Objective Systems Pty Ltd, 2006), 75.
2. Adrian Rogers, *Adrianisms: The Wit and Wisdom of Adrian Rogers* (Memphis: Love Worth Finding Ministries, 2006), 57.

Chapter 8

1. Jason C. Dukes, *Live Sent: You Are a Letter* (Birmingham: New Hope Publishers, 2011), 12.
2. Andrew Murray, *The Believer's New Life* (eBook: Lulu.com, 2007), 129.
3. Ed Stetzer and Philip Nation, eds., "A Passion for Lost Souls," in *The Mission of God Study Bible* (Nashville: Holman Bible Publishers, 2012), 996.

Chapter 9

1. Francis A. Schaeffer, *The Mark of the Christian*, in *The Complete Works of Francis A. Schaeffer*, vol. 4 (Wheaton: Crossway, 1982), 187.
2. Rick Warren, *The Purpose Driven Life* (eBook: Zondervan, 2008).
3. Corrie ten Boom, "I'm Still Learning to Forgive," *Guideposts* (1972); quoted in "Corrie ten Boom (1892-1983)," tlogical [online; cited 13 September 2012]. Available from the Internet: *www.tlogical.net*.

Chapter 10

1. Augustine, "On the Grace of Christ," in *Basic Writings of Saint Augustine*, vol. 1, part 2 (eBook: Kessinger Publishing, 2006), 589.
2. Billy Graham, "Have You Heard the Good News of Salvation?" Billy Graham Evangelistic Association [online], 27 August 2010 [cited 23 August 2012]. Available from the Internet: *www.billygraham.org*.
3. Arthur Bennett, ed., *The Valley of Vision* (Carlisle, PA: The Banner of Truth Trust, 1975), 42-43.

Chapter 11

1. Richard Baxter, *The Reformed Pastor*, ed. William Brown (London: The Religious Tract Society), 19.
2. Timothy Z. Witmer, *The Shepherd Leader* (Phillipsburg, NJ: P&R Publishing, 2010), 13.
3. N. M. Knapp, Letter to Abraham Lincoln, 14 May 1860, in *The Real Lincoln*, by Jesse William Weik (New York: Houghton Mifflin Company, 1922), 263.
4. Martin Luther, "A Sacristy Prayer," in *Through the Year with Martin Luther* (Peabody, MA: Hendrickson, 2007), back cover.

Chapter 12

1. Joni Eareckson Tada, "Hope...the Best of Things," from *Suffering and the Sovereignty of God*, eds. John Piper and Justin Taylor (Wheaton: Crossway, 2006), 194.
2. W. A. Criswell, "Perseverance," Criswell Sermon Library [online], 1974 [cited 30 August 2012]. Available from the Internet: *dev.wacriswell.com*.
3. Arthur Bennett, ed., *The Valley of Vision* (Carlisle, PA: The Banner of Truth Trust, 1975), 59.

Chapter 13

1. J. C. Ryle, *Expository Thoughts on the Gospels: St. Luke, Volume 2* (London: Wertheim, Macintosh, & Hunt, 1859), 239.
2. N. T. Wright, *Surprised by Hope* (New York: HarperOne, 2008), 105-106.

Small Group Tips

Reading through this section and utilizing the suggested principles and practices will greatly enhance the group experience. First is to accept your limitations. You cannot transform a life. Your group must be devoted to the Bible, the Holy Spirit, and the power of Christian community. In doing so your group will have all the tools necessary to draw closer to God and to each other—and to experience heart transformation.

General Tips

• Prepare for each meeting by reviewing the material, praying for each group member, and asking the Holy Spirit to work through you as you point to Jesus each week.

• Make new attendees feel welcome.

• Think of ways to connect with group members away from group time. The amount of participation you have during your group meetings is directly related to the amount of time you connect with your group members away from the group meeting. Consider sending e-mails, texts, or social networking messages encouraging members in their personal devotion times prior to the session.

Materials Needed

• Bible

• Bible study book

• Pen/pencil

Provide Resources for Guests

An inexpensive way to make first-time guests feel welcome is to provide them a copy of your Bible study book. Estimate how many first-time guests you can expect during the course of your study, and secure that number of books. What about people who have not yet visited your group? You can encourage them to visit by providing a copy of the Bible study book.

How to Use This Resource

Welcome to *The Gospel Project*, a gospel-centered curriculum that dives deep into the things of God, lifts up Jesus, focuses on the grand story of Scripture, and drives participants to be on mission. This short-term resource provides opportunities to study the Bible and to encounter the living Christ. *The Gospel Project* provides you with tools and resources to purposefully study God's Word and to grow in the faith and knowledge of God's Son. And what's more, you can do so in the company of others, encouraging and building up one another.

Here are some things to remember that will help you maximize the usefulness of this resource:

Gather a Group. We grow in the faith best in community with other believers, as we love, encourage, correct, and challenge one another. The life of a disciple of Christ was never meant to be lived alone, in isolation.

Pray. Pray regularly for your group members.

Prepare. This resource includes the Bible study content, three devotionals, and follow-up questions for each chapter. Work through the chapter and devotionals in preparation for each group session. Take notes and record your own questions. Also consider the follow-up questions so you are ready to participate in and add to the discussion, bringing up your own notes and questions where appropriate.

Resource Yourself. Make good use of the additional resources available on the Web at *www.gospelproject.com/additionalresources*. Download a podcast. Read a blog post. Be intentional about learning from others in the faith.

Group Time. Gather together with your group to discuss the chapter and devotional content. Work through the follow-up questions and your own questions. Discuss the material and the implications for the lives of believers and the mission to which we have been called.

Overflow. Remember…*The Gospel Project* is not just a curriculum. WE are the project. The gospel is working on us. Don't let your preparation time be simply about the content. Let the truths of God's Word soak in as you study. Let God work on your heart first, and then pray that He will change the hearts of the other people in your group.

New Testament Timeline

circa 4 B.C.–A.D. 9

Place: Bethlehem, Egypt, Nazareth, Jerusalem

Important People: Mary, Joseph, John the Baptizer, Jesus, Herod the Great

Important Events: John the Baptizer's birth; Jesus' incarnation; Jesus' birth; Herod's murder of young male children in Bethlehem; 12-year-old Jesus at the temple

Books that cover this period of history: Matthew; Luke; John

circa 27-30

Place: Nazareth, Galilee, Capernaum, Jerusalem

Important People: John the Baptizer, Jesus, 12 disciples

Important Events: Jesus' baptism; Jesus' temptation; Jesus' teachings

Books that cover this period of history: Matthew; Mark; Luke; John

circa 27-30

Place: Nazareth, Galilee, Capernaum, Jerusalem

Important People: Jesus, 12 disciples, blind Bartimaeus, Gadarene demoniac, Lazarus

Important Events: Jesus' miracles; Jesus' transfiguration

Books that cover this period of history: Matthew; Mark; Luke; John

circa 30

Place: Caesarea Philippi, Jerusalem

Important People: Jesus, Judas, Peter, Pilate, Sanhedrin

Important Events: Triumphal entry; cleansing of temple; Judas' betrayal; Passover supper; Jesus' arrest, trial, and crucifixion

Books that cover this period of history: Matthew; Mark; Luke; John

circa 30

Place: Jerusalem

Important People: Jesus, Peter, John, Pilate, Mary Magdalene

Important Events: Resurrection; post-resurrection appearances; Great Commission; ascension

Books that cover this period of history: Matthew; Mark; Luke; John; Acts

circa 30

Place: Jerusalem

Important People: Peter, John, Stephen

Important Events: Ascension; coming of Holy Spirit at Pentecost; Peter and John's witness; Stephen as first martyr; Paul's conversion

Books that cover this period of history: Acts

circa 30-50

Place: Jerusalem, Antioch, Galatia

Important People: James, Paul, Peter

Important Events: Conversion of Paul; Paul's first missionary journey; the Jerusalem Council

Books that cover this period of history: Acts; Galatians; James

circa 30-60

Place: Jerusalem, Antioch, Corinth, Ephesus

Important People: Disciples, Peter, Paul, Barnabas, Silas, Cornelius, Philip

Important Events: Ascension; Stephen as first martyr; Paul's conversion; Paul's second and third missionary journeys

Books that cover this period of history: Acts; 1–2 Corinthians

Early 60s

Place: Rome, Philippi, Colossae, Ephesus

Important People: Paul, Philemon, Onesimus, Epaphras

Important Events: Paul imprisoned in Rome

Books that cover this period of history:
Ephesians; Philippians; Colossians; Philemon

50s-60s

Place: Gospel spreading throughout the Roman Empire

Important People: Paul, Peter, James, John

Important Events: Paul's missionary journeys; Paul's first Roman imprisonment

Books that cover this period of history: Romans; Hebrews

circa 62-67

Place: Paul's further mission work around the Mediterranean and his final imprisonment in Rome

Important People: Paul, Timothy, Titus, Lois, Eunice, Demas, Prisca, Aquila

Important Events: Paul's final missionary journey; Paul's final imprisonment

Books that cover this period of history: 1–2 Timothy; Titus

circa 62-90

Place: Rome, Ephesus, Asia Minor

Important People: Peter, John

Important Events: Persecution against Christians; Peter's martyrdom; destruction of Jerusalem; John as spiritual leader in Ephesus

Books that cover this period of history: 1–2 Peter; 1–3 John

50s-90s

Place: Thessalonica, Ephesus, Patmos

Important People: Paul, Jude, John

Important Events: John's vision of the future

Books that cover this period of history:
1–2 Thessalonians; Jude; Revelation

God's Story Continues...

Enjoying *The Gospel Project*? If your group meets regularly, you might consider adopting *The Gospel Project* as an ongoing Bible study series.

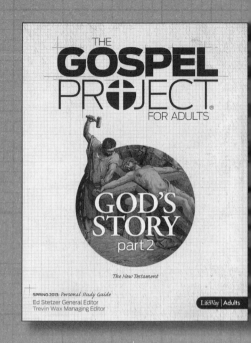

Reasons to switch to ongoing studies

Consistency: The ongoing format helps ensure that you will be fully established in a gospel-centered understanding of the entire Bible. As you move through *The Gospel Project*, you can rest assured that you are receiving robust biblical teaching all year long.

Community: When you join thousands of other groups working through the same topics at the same time, you receive the benefit of online interaction through *The Gospel Project* blog.

Cost: Jumping in with our ongoing format is the most affordable option over time.

The Gospel Project is available for kids, students, and adults so that your entire church family can explore the grand narrative of redemption history together. Available in print and digital formats, it is easy to choose the option that works best for you. For more information on *The Gospel Project* and to order, visit *gospelproject.com*.

Web: **gospelproject.com** Twitter: **@Gospel_Project** Facebook: **TheGospelProject**